Minnesota Rules of Civil Proce
With amendments effective January

I. SCOPE OF RULES - ONE FORM OF ACTION

Rule 1. Scope of Rules

Rule 2. One Form of Action

II. COMMENCEMENT OF THE ACTION; SERVICE OF PROCESS, PLEADINGS, MOTIONS, AND ORDERS

Rule 3. Commencement of the Action; Service of the Complaint; Filing of the Action
3.01 Commencement of the Action
3.02 Service of Complaint

Rule 4. Service
4.01 Summons; Form
4.02 By Whom Served
4.03 Personal Service
4.04 Service by Publications; Personal Service Out of State
4.041 Additional Information to be Published
4.042 Service of the Complaint
4.043 Service by Publication; Defendant May Defend; Restitution
4.044 Nonresident Owner of Land Appointing an Agent
4.05 Waiving Service of Summons
4.06 Return
4.07 Amendments

Rule 5. Service and Filing of Pleadings and Other Documents
5.01 Service; When Required; Appearance
5.02 Service; How Made
5.03 Service; Numerous Defendants
5.04 Filing; Certificate of Service
5.05 Filing; Facsimile Transmission
5.06 Filing Electronically

Rule 5A. Notice of Constitutional Challenge to a Statute

Rule 6. Time
6.01 Computation
6.02 Enlargement
6.03 Unaffected by Expiration of Term
6.04 For Motions; Affidavits
6.05 Additional Time After Service by Mail or Service Late in Day [Abrogated]

III. PLEADINGS AND MOTIONS

Rule 7. Pleadings Allowed; Form of Motions
7.01 Pleadings
7.02 Motion and Other Documents

Rule 8. General Rules of Pleading
8.01 Claims for Relief
8.02 Defenses; Form of Denials
8.03 Affirmative Defenses
8.04 Effect of Failure to Deny
8.05 Pleading to be Concise and Direct; Consistency
8.06 Construction of Pleadings

Rule 9. Pleading Special Matters
9.01 Capacity
9.02 Fraud, Mistake, Condition of Mind
9.03 Conditions Precedent
9.04 Official Document or Act
9.05 Judgment
9.06 Time and Place
9.07 Special Damages
9.08 Unknown Party; How Designated

Rule 10. Form of Pleadings
10.01 Caption; Names of Parties
10.02 Paragraph; Separate Statements
10.03 Adoption by Reference; Exhibits
10.04 Failure to Comply

Rule 11. Signing of Pleadings, Motions, and Other Documents; Representations to Court; Sanctions
11.01 Signature
11.02 Representations to Court
11.03 Sanctions
11.04 Inapplicability to Discovery

Rule 12. Defenses and Objections; When and How Presented; By Pleading or Motion; Motion for Judgment on Pleadings
12.01 When Presented
12.02 How Presented
12.03 Motion for Judgment on the Pleadings
12.04 Preliminary Hearing
12.05 Motion for More Definite Statement, for Paragraphing and for Separate Statement
12.06 Motion to Strike
12.07 Consolidation of Defenses in Motion

12.08 Waiver or Preservation of Certain Defenses

Rule 13. Counterclaim and Cross-Claim
13.01 Compulsory Counterclaims
13.02 Permissive Counterclaims
13.03 Counterclaim Exceeding Opposing Claim
13.04 Counterclaim Against the State of Minnesota
13.05 Counterclaim Maturing or Acquired After Pleading
13.06 Omitted Counterclaim
13.07 Cross-Claim against Co-Party
13.08 Joinder of Additional Parties
13.09 Separate Trials; Separate Judgment

Rule 14. Third-Party Practice
14.01 When A Defending Party May Bring in Third Party
14.02 Third-Party Defendant's Claims and Defenses
14.03 Plaintiff's Claims Against A Third-Party Defendant
14.04 Motion to Strike, Sever, or Try Separately
14.05 Third-Party Defendant's Claim Against a Nonparty
14.06 When a Plaintiff May Bring in a Third Party
14.07 Defending Against a Demand for Judgment for the Plaintiff
14.08 Protective Orders for Parties and Prevention of Delay

Rule 15. Amended and Supplemental Pleadings
15.01 Amendments
15.02 Amendments to Conform to the Evidence
15.03 Relation Back of Amendments
15.04 Supplemental Pleadings

Rule 16. Pretrial Conferences; Scheduling; Management
16.01 Pretrial Conferences; Objectives
16.02 Scheduling and Planning
16.03 Subjects for Consideration
16.04 Final Pretrial Conference
16.05 Pretrial Orders
16.06 Sanctions

IV. PARTIES

Rule 17. Parties Plaintiff and Defendant; Capacity
17.01 Real Party in Interest
17.02 Infants or Incompetent Persons

Rule 18. Joinder of Claims and Remedies
18.01 Joinder of Claims
18.02 Joinder of Remedies; Fraudulent Conveyances

Rule 19. Joinder of Persons Needed for Just Adjudication
19.01 Persons to be Joined if Feasible
19.02 Determination by Court Whenever Joinder not Feasible
19.03 Pleading Reasons for Nonjoinder
19.04 Exception of Class Actions

Rule 20. Permissive Joinder of Parties
20.01 Permissive Joinder
20.02 Separate Trials

Rule 21. Misjoinder and Nonjoinder of Parties

Rule 22. Interpleader

Rule 23. Class Actions
23.01 Prerequisites to a Class Action
23.02 Class Actions Maintainable
23.03 Determining by Order Whether to Certify a Class Action; Appointing Class Counsel; Notice and Membership in Class; Judgment; Multiple Classes and Subclasses
23.04 Orders in Conduct of Actions
23.05 Settlement, Voluntary Dismissal , Compromise
23.06 Appeals
23.07 Class Counsel
23.08 Attorney Fees Award
23.09 Derivative Actions by Shareholders or Members
23.10 Actions Relating to Unincorporated Associations

Rule 24. Intervention
24.01 Intervention of Right
24.02 Permissive Intervention
24.03 Procedure
24.04 Notice to Attorney General

Rule 25. Substitution of Parties
25.01 Death
25.02 Incompetency
25.03 Transfer of Interest
25.04 Public Officers; Death or Separation from Office

V. DEPOSITIONS AND DISCOVERY

Rule 26. Duty to Disclose; General Provisions Governing Discovery
26.01 Required Disclosures
26.02 Discovery Methods, Scope and Limits
26.03 Protective Orders

26.04 Timing and Sequence of Discovery
26.05 Supplementation of Responses
26.06 Discovery Conference and Discovery Plan
26.07 Signing of Discovery Requests, Responses and Objections

Rule 27. Deposition before Action or Pending Appeal
27.01 Before Action
27.02 Pending Appeal
27.03 Perpetuation by Action

Rule 28. Persons Before Whom Depositions May Be Taken
28.01 Within the United States
28.02 In Foreign Countries
28.03 Disqualification for Interest

Rule 29. Stipulations Regarding Discovery Procedure

Rule 30. Depositions Upon Oral Examination
30.01 When Depositions May Be Taken
30.02 Notice of Examination; General Requirements; Special Notice; Non-Stenographic Method of Recording; Production of Documents and Things; Deposition of Organization; Depositions by Telephone
30.03 Examination and Cross-Examination; Record of Examination; Oath; Objections
30.04 Schedule and Duration; Motion to Terminate or Limit Examination
30.05 Review by Witness; Changes; Signing
30.06 Certification and Filing by Officer; Exhibits; Copies; Notices of Filing
30.07 Failure to Attend or to Serve Subpoena; Expenses

Rule 31. Depositions of Witnesses Upon Written Questions
31.01 Serving Questions; Notice
31.02 Officers to Take Responses and Prepare Record
31.03 Notice of Filing

Rule 32. Use of Depositions in Court Proceedings
32.01 Use of Depositions
32.02 Objections to Admissibility
32.03 Form of Presentation
32.04 Effect of Errors and Irregularities in Depositions
32.05 Use of Video Depositions

Rule 33. Interrogatories to Parties
33.01 Availability
33.02 Scope; Use at Trial
33.03 Option to Produce Business Records

Rule 34. Production of Documents, Electronically Stored Information, and Things and Entry Upon Land for Inspection and Other Purposes
34.01 Scope
34.02 Procedure
34.03 Persons Not Parties

Rule 35. Physical, Mental and Blood Examination of Persons
35.01 Order of Examinations
35.02 Report of Findings
35.03 Waiver of Medical Privilege
35.04 Medical Disclosures and Depositions of Medical Experts

Rule 36. Requests for Admission
36.01 Request for Admission
36.02 Effect of Admission

Rule 37. Failure to Make Disclosures or To Cooperate in Discovery: Sanctions
37.01 Motion for Order Compelling Disclosure or Discovery
37.02 Failure to Comply with Order
37.03 Failure to Disclose, to Supplement an Earlier Response, or to Admit
37.04 Failure of a Party to Attend at Own Deposition or Serve Answers
37.05 Failure to Preserve Electronically Stored Information
37.06 Failure to Participate in Framing a Discovery Plan

VI. TRIALS

Rule 38. Jury Trial of Right
38.01 Right Preserved
38.02 Waiver
38.03 Placing Action on Calendar

Rule 39. Trial by Jury or by the Court
39.01 By Court
39.02 Advisory Jury and Trial by Consent
39.03 Preliminary Instructions in Jury Trials
39.04 Opening Statements by Counsel

Rule 40. Assignment of Cases for Trial

Rule 41. Dismissal of Actions
41.01 Voluntary Dismissal; Effect Thereof
41.02 Involuntary Dismissal; Effect Thereof
41.03 Dismissal of Counterclaim, Cross-Claim, or Third-Party Claim
41.04 Costs of Previously Dismissed Action

Rule 42. Separate Trials
42.01 Consolidation
42.02 Separate Trials

Rule 43. Taking of Testimony
43.01 Form
43.02 [Abrogated]
43.03 [Abrogated]
43.04 Affirmation in Lieu of Oath
43.05 Evidence and Motions
43.06 [Abrogated]
43.07 Interpreters

Rule 44. Proof of Official Record
44.01 Authentication
44.02 Lack of Record
44.03 Other Proof
44.04 Determination of Foreign Law [Abrogated]

Rule 45. Subpoena
45.01 For Attendance of Witnesses; Form; Issuance
45.02 Service
45.03 Protection of Persons Subject to Subpoenas
45.04 Duties in Responding to Subpoena
45.05 Contempt
45.06 Interstate Depositions and Discovery

Rule 46. Exceptions Unnecessary

Rule 47. Jurors
47.01 Examination of Jurors
47.02 Alternate Jurors [Abrogated]
47.03 Separation of Jury
47.04 Excuse

Rule 48. Number of Jurors; Participation in Verdict

Rule 49. Special Verdicts and Interrogatories
49.01 Special Verdicts
49.02 General Verdict Accompanied by Answer to Interrogatories

Rule 50. Judgment as a Matter of Law in Jury Trials; Alternative Motion for New Trial; Conditional Rulings
50.01 Judgment as a Matter of Law
50.02 Renewing Motion for Judgment After Trial; Alternative Motion for New Trial

50.03 Granting Renewed Motion for Judgment as a Matter of Law; Conditional Rulings; New Trial Motion
50.04 Denial of Motion for Judgment as a Matter of Law

Rule 51. Instructions to the Jury; Objections; Preserving a Claim of Error
51.01 Requests
51.02 Instructions
51.03 Objections
51.04 Assigning Error; Plain Error

Rule 52. Findings by the Court
52.01 Effect
52.02 Amendment

Rule 53. Masters
53.01 Appointment
53.02 Order Appointing Master
53.03 Master's Authority
53.04 Evidentiary Hearings
53.05 Master's Orders
53.06 Master's Reports
53.07 Action on Master's Order, Report, or Recommendations
53.08 Compensation
53.09 Appointment of Statutory Referee

Rule 54. Judgments; Costs
54.01 Definition; Form
54.02 Judgment upon Multiple Claims
54.03 Demand for Judgment
54.04 Costs

Rule 55. Default
55.01 Judgment
55.02 Plaintiffs; Counterclaimants; Cross-Claimants

Rule 56. Summary Judgment
56.01 Motion for Summary Judgment or Partial Summary Judgment
56.02 Time to File a Motion
56.03 Procedures
56.04 When Facts Are Unavailable to the Nonmovant
56.05 Failing to Properly Support or Address a Fact
56.06 Judgment Independent of the Motion
56.07 Failing to Grant All the Requested Relief
56.08 Affidavit Submitted in Bad Faith

Rule 57. Declaratory Judgments

Rule 58. Entry of Judgment; Stay
58.01 Entry
58.02 Stay

Rule 59. New Trials
59.01 Grounds
59.02 Basis of Motion
59.03 Time for Motion
59.04 Time for Serving Affidavits
59.05 On Initiative of Court
59.06 Stay of Entry of Judgment

Rule 60. Relief from Judgment or Order
60.01 Clerical Mistakes
60.02 Mistakes; Inadvertence; Excusable Neglect; Newly Discovered Evidence; Fraud; etc.

Rule 61. Harmless Error

Rule 62. Stay of Proceedings to Enforce a Judgment
62.01 Stay on Motions
62.02 Injunction Pending Appeal
62.03 Stay upon Appeal
62.04 Stay in Favor of the State or Agency Thereof
62.05 Power of Appellate Court Not Limited
62.06 Stay of Judgment Upon Multiple Claims

Rule 63. Disability or Disqualification of Judge; Notice to Remove; Assignment of a Judge
63.01 Disability of Judge
63.02 Interest or Bias
63.03 Notice to Remove
63.04 Assignment of Judge

VII. PROVISIONAL AND FINAL REMEDIES AND SPECIAL PROCEEDINGS

Rule 64. Seizure of Person or Property

Rule 65. Injunctions
65.01 Temporary Restraining Order; Notice; Hearing; Duration
65.02 Temporary Injunction
65.03 Security
65.04 Form and Scope of Injunction or Restraining Order

Rule 66. Receivers

Rule 67. Deposit in Court

67.01 In an Action
67.02 When No Action is Brought
67.03 Court May Order Deposit or Seizure of Property
67.04 Money Paid into Court

Rule 68. Offer of Judgment or Settlement
68.01 Offer
68.02 Acceptance or Rejection of Offer
68.03 Effect of Unaccepted Offer
68.04 Applicable Attorney Fees and Prejudgment Interest

Rule 69. Execution

Rule 70. Judgment for Specific Acts; Vesting Title

Rule 71. Process in Behalf of and Against Persons Not Parties

Rules 72 to 76. (Reserved for Future Use.)

VIII. DISTRICT COURTS AND COURT ADMINISTRATORS

Rule 77. District Courts and Court Administrators
77.01 District Courts Always Open
77.02 Trials and Hearings; Orders in Chambers
77.03 Court Administrator's Office and Orders by Court Administrator
77.04 Notice of Orders or Judgments

Rules 78 and 79. (Reserved for Future Use.)

Rule 80. Stenographic Report or Transcript as Evidence

Rule 81. Applicability; in General
81.01 Statutory and Other Procedures
81.02 Appeals to District Courts
81.03 Rules Incorporated into Statutes

Rule 82. Jurisdiction and Venue

Rule 83. Rules by District Courts

Rule 84. Appendix of Forms

Rule 85. Title

Rule 86. Effective Date
86.01 Effective Date and Application to Pending Proceedings

I. SCOPE OF RULES - ONE FORM OF ACTION

RULE 1. SCOPE OF RULES

These rules govern the procedure in the district courts of the State of Minnesota in all suits of a civil nature, with the exceptions stated in Rule 81. They shall be construed and administered to secure the just, speedy, and inexpensive determination of every action.

It is the responsibility of the court and the parties to examine each civil action to assure that the process and the costs are proportionate to the amount in controversy and the complexity and importance of the issues. The factors to be considered by the court in making a proportionality assessment include, without limitation: needs of the case, amount in controversy, parties' resources, and complexity and importance of the issues at stake in the litigation.

(Amended effective July 1, 2013.)

Advisory Committee Comments--1996 Amendments

This change conforms the rule to its federal counterpart. The amendment is intended to make clear that the goals of just, speedy, and inexpensive resolution of litigation are just as important--if not more important--in questions that do not involve interpretation of the rules. These goals should guide all aspects of judicial administration, and this amendment expressly so states.

RULE 2. ONE FORM OF ACTION

There shall be one form of action to be known as "civil action."

II. COMMENCEMENT OF THE ACTION; SERVICE OF PROCESS, PLEADINGS, MOTIONS, AND ORDERS

RULE 3. COMMENCEMENT OF THE ACTION; SERVICE OF THE COMPLAINT; FILING OF THE ACTION

3.01. Commencement of the Action

A civil action is commenced against each defendant:
(a) when the summons is served upon that defendant, or
(b) at the date of signing of a waiver of service pursuant to Rule 4.05; or
(c) when the summons is delivered for service to the sheriff in the county where the defendant resides personally, by U.S. Mail (postage prepaid), or by commercial courier with proof of delivery, or by electronic means consented to by the sheriff's office either in writing or electronically; but such delivery shall be ineffectual unless within 60 days thereafter the summons is actually served on that defendant or the first publication thereof is made.

Filing requirements are set forth in Rule 5.04, which requires filing with the court within one year after commencement for non-family cases.

(Amended effective September 1, 2020.)

Advisory Committee Comments—2015 Amendments

This rule is amended to add the explicit provision for consent to service by any means in subdivision (b), not only service by mail. If the party to be served consents to service, the service is effective and constitutionally sound regardless of method. Thus, a party may consent to service by ordinary electronic mail even though the rules do not otherwise provide for it.

Advisory Committee Comment—2018 Amendments

Rule 3.01 is amended to implement the amendment to Rule 4.05, which replaces the somewhat unreliable procedure involving the "Acknowledgement of Service" form with a more straightforward procedure relying on a "Waiver of Service" form. Rule 3.01 defines the date of commencement of an action using the wavier of process procedure.

Advisory Committee Comments-2020 Amendments

Rule 3.01 is amended to clarify the forms of delivery to sheriffs that may be used to commence an action. It does not restrict or change how service on the defendant is accomplished. The committee expects that most sheriffs will make available on their websites or will provide information upon inquiry as to how they prefer to receive requests for service under this rule. Transmittal by U.S. Mail is expressly authorized, and a party may use Certified Mail, Return Receipt Requested in order to obtain proof of receipt. The rule also authorizes delivery to the sheriff by commercial courier (e.g., Federal Express, UPS), which may be most effective in getting the required documents in the sheriff's hands and would also create a record of delivery (although the rule does not require a proof of delivery).

The amended rule intentionally does not authorize delivery to the sheriff in the proper county by facsimile. As anachronistic and inconvenient as facsimile is for most purposes in 2020, it is particularly ill-suited for this purpose. Minn. R. Civ. P. 3.02 requires service of the complaint with the summons and that may result in lengthy facsimile transmissions. Moreover, faxes impose undue burdens on sheriffs' offices. Sheriffs in most counties will accept delivery by hand delivery, U.S. Mail, commercial courier, or email to a designated email address.

3.02. Service of Complaint

A copy of the complaint shall be served with the summons, except when the service is by publication as provided in Rule 4.04.

RULE 4. SERVICE

4.01. Summons; Form

The summons shall state the name of the court and the names of the parties, be subscribed by the plaintiff or by the plaintiff's attorney, give an address within the state where the subscriber may be served in person and by mail, state the time within which these rules require the defendant to serve an answer, and notify the defendant that if the defendant fails to do so judgment by default will be rendered against the defendant or the relief demanded in the complaint.

4.02. By Whom Served

Unless otherwise ordered by the court, the sheriff or any other person not less than 18 years of age and not a party to the action, may make service of a summons or other process.

4.03. Personal Service

Service of summons within the state shall be as follows:

(a) **Upon an Individual.** Upon an individual by delivering a copy to the individual personally or by leaving a copy at the individual's usual place of abode with some person of suitable age and discretion then residing therein.

If the individual has, pursuant to statute, consented to any other method of service or appointed an agent to receive service of summons, or if a statute designates a state official to receive service of summons, service may be made in the manner provided by such statute.

If the individual is confined to a state institution, by serving also the chief executive officer at the institution.

If the individual is an infant under the age of 14 years, by serving also the individual's father or mother, and if neither is within the state, then a resident guardian if the infant has one known to the plaintiff, and if the infant has none, then the person having control of such defendant, or with whom the infant resides, or by whom the infant is employed.

(b) **Upon Partnerships and Associations.** Upon a partnership or association which is subject to suit under a common name, by delivering a copy to a member or the managing agent of the partnership or association. If the partnership or association has, pursuant to statute, consented to any other method of service or appointed an agent to receive service of summons, or if a statute designates a state official to receive service of summons, service may be made in the manner provided by such statute.

(c) **Upon a Corporation.** Upon a domestic or foreign corporation, by delivering a copy to an officer or managing agent, or to any other agent authorized expressly or impliedly or designated by statute to receive service of summons, and if the agent is one authorized or designated under statute to receive service any statutory provision for the manner of such service shall be complied with. In the case of a transportation or express corporation, the summons may be served by delivering a copy to any ticket, freight, or soliciting agent found in the county in which the action is brought, and if such corporation is a foreign corporation and has no such agent in the county in which the plaintiff elects to bring the action, then upon any such agent of the corporation within the state.

(d) **Upon the State.** Upon the state by delivering a copy to the attorney general, a deputy attorney general or an assistant attorney general.

(e) **Upon Public Corporation.** Upon a municipal or other public corporation by delivering a copy
    (1) To the chair of the county board or to the county auditor of a defendant county;
    (2) To the chief executive officer or to the clerk of a defendant city, village or borough;
    (3) To the chair of the town board or to the clerk of a defendant town;
    (4) To any member of the board or other governing body of a defendant school district; or
    (5) To any member of the board or other governing body of a defendant public board or public body not hereinabove enumerated.

If service cannot be made as provided in this Rule 4.03(e), the court may direct the manner of such service.

4.04. Service by Publications; Personal Service Out of State

(a) **Service by Publications.** Service by publication shall be sufficient to confer jurisdiction:
    (1) When the defendant is a resident individual domiciliary having departed from the state with intent to defraud creditors, or to avoid service, or remains concealed therein with the like intent;
    (2) When the plaintiff has acquired a lien upon property or credits within the state by attachment or garnishment, and
        (A) The defendant is a resident individual who has departed from the state, or cannot be found therein, or
        (B) The defendant is a nonresident individual or a foreign corporation, partnership or association;
    When quasi in rem jurisdiction has been obtained, a party defending the action thereby submits personally to the jurisdiction of the court. An appearance solely to contest the validity of quasi in rem jurisdiction is not such a submission.

(3) When the action is for marriage dissolution or separate maintenance and the court has ordered service by published notice;

(4) When the subject of the action is real or personal property within the state in or upon which the defendant has or claims a lien or interest, or the relief demanded consists wholly or partly in excluding the defendant from any such interest or lien;

(5) When the action is to foreclose a mortgage or to enforce a lien on real estate within the state.

The summons may be served by three weeks' published notice in any of the cases enumerated herein when the complaint and an affidavit of the plaintiff or the plaintiff's attorney have been filed with the court. The affidavit shall state the existence of one of the enumerated cases, and that the affiant believes the defendant is not a resident of the state or cannot be found therein, and either that the affiant has mailed a copy of the summons to the defendant at the defendant's place of residence or that such residence is not known to the affiant. The service of the summons shall be deemed complete 21 days after the first publication.

(b) **Personal Service Outside State.** Personal service of such summons outside the state, proved by the affidavit of the person making the same, shall have the same effect as the published notice provided for herein.

(c) **Service Outside United States.** Unless otherwise provided by law, service upon an individual, other than an infant or an incompetent person, may be effected in a place not within the state:

(1) by any internationally agreed means reasonably calculated to give notice, such as those means authorized by the Hague Convention on the Service Abroad of Judicial and Extrajudicial Documents; or

(2) if there is no internationally agreed means of service or the applicable international agreement allows other means of service, provided that service is reasonably calculated to give notice;

 (A) in the manner prescribed by the law of the foreign country for service in that country in an action in any of its courts of general jurisdiction; or

 (B) as directed by the foreign authority in response to a letter rogatory or letter of request; or

 (C) unless prohibited by the law of the foreign country, by
  (i) delivery to the individual personally of a copy of the summons and the complaint; or
  (ii) any form of mail requiring a signed receipt, to be addressed and dispatched by the court administrator to the party to be served; or

(3) by other means not prohibited by international agreement as may be directed by the court.

(Amended effective July 1, 2015.)

Advisory Committee Comments—1996 Amendments

Rule 4.04 is amended to conform the rule to its federal counterpart, in part. The new provision adopts verbatim the provisions for service of process outside the United States contained in the federal rules. This modification is appropriate because this subject is handled well by the federal rule and because it is advantageous to have the two rules similar. This is particularly valuable given the dearth of state-court authority on foreign service of process. Existing portions of the rule are renumbered for clarity.

Advisory Committee Comments—2015 Amendments

Rule 4.04 is amended to implement a new statute directing the courts to accept documents without notarization if they are signed under the following language: "I declare under penalty of perjury that everything I have stated in this document is true and correct." Minn. Stat. § 358.116 (2014) (codifying 2014 Minn. Laws ch. 204, § 3). The statute allows the courts to require specifically, by rule, that notarization is necessary. The difficulty in accomplishing and documenting notarization for documents that are e-filed and e-served militates against requiring formal notarization, and notarization often places a significant burden on self-represented litigants. Rule 15 of the Minnesota General Rules of Practice provides that documents signed in accordance with its terms constitute "affidavits." Rule 15 of the Minnesota General Rules of Practice establishes uniform requirements for the formalities of documents signed under penalty of perjury.

4.041. Additional Information to be Published

In all cases where publication of summons is made in an action in which the title to, or any interest in or lien upon, real property is involved or affected or is brought in question, the publication shall also contain a description of the real property involved, affected or brought in question thereby, and a statement of the object of the action. No other notice of the pendency of the action need be published.

4.042. Service of the Complaint

If the defendant shall appear within 14 days after the completion of service by publication, the plaintiff, within 7 days after such appearance, shall serve the complaint, by copy, on the defendant or the defendant's attorney. The defendant shall then have at least 21 days in which to answer the same.

(Amended effective January 1, 2020.)

Advisory Committee Comment—2020 Amendments

Rule 4.042 is amended as part of the extensive amendments made to the timing provisions of the rules. These amendments implement the adoption of a standard "day" for counting deadlines under the rules—counting all days regardless of the length of the period and standardizing the time periods, where practicable, to a 7-, 14-, 21- or 28-day schedule.

The amendment to Rule 4.042 also lengthens the time to respond to a Complaint served following service of the Summons by publication to 21 days. This is the same period a party has following other forms of service of the Complaint, and there is no reason to require a shorter period. See Rule 12.01. This amendment is intended to obviate at least some motions for extension of the time to answer that are encountered under the shorter deadline in the previous rule.

4.043. Service by Publication; Defendant May Defend; Restitution

If the summons is served by publication, and the defendant receives no actual notification of the action, the defendant shall be permitted to defend upon application to the court before judgment and for sufficient cause; and, except in an action for marriage dissolution, the defendant, in like manner, may be permitted to defend at any time within one year after judgment, on such terms as may be just. If the defense is sustained, and any part of the judgment has been enforced, such restitution shall be made as the court may direct.

4.044. Nonresident Owner of Land Appointing an Agent

If a nonresident person or corporation owning or claiming any interest or lien in or upon lands in the state appoints an agent pursuant to Minnesota Statutes, section 557.01, service of summons in an action involving such real estate shall be made upon the agent or the principal in accordance with Rule 4.03, and service by publication shall not be made upon the principal.

4.05. Waiving Service of Summons

(a) Requesting a Waiver. An individual, corporation, or association that is subject to service under Rule 4.03 has a duty to avoid unnecessary expenses of serving the summons. A plaintiff may request that the defendant waive service of a summons. The notice and request must:
(1) be in writing and be addressed:
(A) to the individual defendant; or
(B) for a defendant subject to service under Rule 4.03(b)-(e) to the agent authorized to receive service;
(2) be accompanied by a copy of the complaint, two copies of Form 22B or a substantially similar form, and a prepaid means for returning a signed copy of the form;
(3) inform a defendant, using Form 22B or a substantially similar form, of the consequences of waiving and not waiving service;
(4) state the date when the request is sent;
(5) give a defendant 30 days after the request was sent—or 60 days if sent to a defendant outside the United States—to return the waiver; and
(6) be sent by first-class mail or other reliable means.

(b) Failure to Waive. If a defendant located within the United States fails, without good cause, to sign and return a waiver requested by a plaintiff located within the United States, the court must impose on the defendant:
(1) the expenses later incurred in making service; and
(2) the reasonable expenses, including attorney's fees, of any motion required to collect those service expenses.

(c) Time to Answer After a Waiver. A defendant who, before being served with process, timely returns a signed waiver need not serve an answer to the complaint until 60 days after the request was sent to that defendant—or until 90 days after it was sent to that defendant outside the United States.

(d) Results of Filing of a Waiver. When a plaintiff files a waiver of service, proof of service is not required and these rules apply as if a summons and complaint had been served on the date of signing of the waiver.

(e) Jurisdiction and Venue Not Waived. Waiving service of a summons does not waive any objection to personal jurisdiction or to venue.

(Amended effective July 1, 2018.)

Advisory Committee Comment—2018 Amendments

Rule 4.05 is completely revamped to replace the somewhat unreliable procedure relying on the "Acknowledgement of Service" form with a more straightforward procedure, used in federal court since 1993, relying on a "Waiver of Service" form. New Rule 4.05 is modeled closely on its federal counterpart.

The former procedure created the illusion that valid service could be accomplished by U.S. Mail, but it was a procedure that gave control over the process completely to the defendant and little incentive to a plaintiff to make use of it. This rule does not authorize service by mere mailing—it is necessary for the defendant to waive formal service and return the waiver-of-service form. Service is accomplished and proven by the waiver, not the mailing. Additionally, the new procedure is not limited to delivery by mail or any other means expressly authorized by these rules—it allows valid service to be accomplished by any means that is agreed to the defendant being served—mail, private courier, email, or even social media would all be acceptable if the defendant agreed to waive service under this rule. The only requirement is that the defendant sign and return a waiver-of-service form.

4.06. Return

Service of summons and other process shall be proved by the certificate of the sheriff or other peace officer making it, by the affidavit of any other person making it, by the written admission or acknowledgment of the party served, or if served by publication, by the affidavit of the printer or the printer's designee. The proof of service in all cases other than by published notice shall state the time, place, and manner of service. Failure to make proof of service shall not affect the validity of the service.

(Amended effective August 1, 2000.)

4.07. Amendments

The court in its discretion and on such terms as it deems just may at any time allow any summons or other process or proof of service thereof to be amended, unless it clearly appears that substantial rights of the person against whom the process issued would be prejudiced thereby.

RULE 5. SERVICE AND FILING OF PLEADINGS AND OTHER DOCUMENTS

5.01. Service; When Required; Appearance

Except as otherwise provided in these rules, every order required by its terms to be served, every pleading subsequent to the original complaint unless the court otherwise orders because of numerous defendants, every written motion other than one which may be heard ex parte, and every written notice, appearance, demand, offer of judgment, designation of record on appeal, and similar document shall be served upon each of the parties. No service need be made on parties in default for failure to appear except that pleadings asserting new or additional claims for relief against them shall be served upon them in the manner provided for service of summons in Rule 4. A party appears when that party serves or files any document in the proceeding.

(Amended effective September 1, 2012.)

5.02. Service; How Made

(a) **Methods of Service.** Whenever under these rules service is required or permitted to be made upon a party represented by an attorney, the service shall be made upon the attorney unless service upon the party is ordered by the court. Written admission of service by the party or the party's attorney shall be sufficient proof of service. If Rule 14 of the General Rules of Practice for the District Courts or an order of the Minnesota Supreme Court authorizes or requires that service be made by electronic means, service shall be made by compliance with subdivision (b) of this rule. Otherwise, service upon the attorney or upon a party shall be made by delivering a copy to the attorney or party; by mailing a copy to the attorney or party at the attorney's or party's last known address; or, if no address is known, by leaving it with the court administrator. Delivery of a copy within this rule means: handing it to the attorney or to the party; or leaving it at the attorney's or party's office with a clerk or other person in charge thereof; or, if there is no one in charge, leaving it in a conspicuous place therein; or, if the office is closed or the person to be served has no office, leaving it at the attorney's or party's dwelling house or usual place of abode with some person of suitable age and discretion then residing therein.

(b) **E-Service.** Service of all documents after the original complaint may, and where required by these rules shall, be made by electronic means as authorized by Rule 14 of the General Rules of Practice for the District Courts.

(c) **Effective Date of Service.** Service by mail is complete upon mailing. Service by facsimile is complete upon completion of the facsimile transmission. Service by authorized electronic means using the court's E-Filing System as defined in Rule 14 of the General Rules of Practice for the District Courts is complete upon completion of the electronic transmission of the document(s) to the E-Filing System.

(d) **Technical Errors; Relief.** Upon satisfactory proof that electronic filing or electronic service of a document was not completed, any party may obtain relief in accordance with Rule 14.01(c) of the General Rules of Practice for the District Courts.

(Amended effective July 1, 2015.)

Advisory Committee Comments—2015 Amendments

Rule 5.02 is amended in several ways to implement the use of e-filing and e-service in civil actions. Rule 5.02(a) adopts the more detailed provisions of Rule 14 of the Minnesota General Rules of Practice, which establishes procedures for e-filing and e-service in all trial courts. See Minn. Gen. R. Prac. 1.01. The deleted reference to filing by facsimile from Rule 5.02(a) is not intended to affect the availability of facsimile service or filing. Facsimile transmission is defined as a means of electronic transmission allowed under Minn. Gen. R. Prac. 14.02(a)(7).

The use of the alternative "may or shall" language in Rule 5.02(a) reflects the expectation that the implementation of electronic filing and service is likely to involve some period of time where e-filing and e-service will be required for some actions (based on district, county, or type of action), permitted for others, or not permitted at all. The applicability of e-filing and e-service to particular actions should be established in separate implementation orders.

5.03. Service: Numerous Defendants

If the defendants are numerous, the court, upon motion or upon its own initiative, may order that service of the pleadings of the defendants and replies thereto need not be made as between the defendants and that any cross-claim, counterclaim, or matter constituting an avoidance or affirmative defense contained therein shall be deemed to be denied or avoided by all other parties and that the filing of any such pleading with the court and service thereof upon the plaintiff constitutes due notice of it to the parties. A copy of every such order shall be served upon the parties in such manner and form as the court directs.

5.04. Filing; Certificate of Service

(a) **Deadline for Filing Action.** Any action that is not filed with the court within one year of commencement against any party is deemed dismissed with prejudice against all parties unless the parties within that year sign a stipulation to extend the filing period. This paragraph does not apply to family cases governed by rules 301 to 378 of the General Rules of Practice for the District Courts.

(b) **Filing of Documents After the Complaint; Certificate of Service.** All documents after the complaint required to be served upon a party, together with a certificate of service specifying the details of how and when service was accomplished and signed under oath or penalty of perjury by the person effecting service, shall be filed with the court within a reasonable time after service, except disclosures under Rule 26, expert disclosures and reports, depositions upon oral examination and interrogatories, requests for documents, requests for admission, and answers and responses thereto shall not be filed unless authorized by court order or rule. If a document is electronically filed and electronically served together using the district court's e-service system, no separate proof of service is required.

(c) **Rejection of Filing.** The administrator shall not refuse to accept for filing any document presented for that purpose solely because it is not presented in proper form as required by these rules or any local rules or practices. Documents may be rejected for filing if:
   (1) tendered without a required filing fee or a correct assigned file number;
   (2) tendered to an administrator other than for the court where the action is pending;
   (3) the document constitutes a discovery request or response submitted without the express permission of the court; or
   (4) the document contains a restricted identifier or other non-public information submitted in violation of Rules 11.02, 11.03, or 11.04 of the General Rules of Practice for the District Courts. This clause (4) shall not apply to criminal, civil commitment, juvenile protection, or juvenile delinquency cases, or to medical records in any type of case.

(d) **Relation Back.** On motion and in the interests of justice, the court may deem a filing rejected under paragraphs (c)(1) and (c)(4) of this rule to be filed as of the time and date it was originally tendered to the appropriate administrator for filing.

(Amended effective January 1, 2021.)

Advisory Committee Comments—2015 Amendments

Rule 5.04 clarifies the limited circumstances where documents tendered to the court administrator for filing can be rejected. These provisions largely reflect current practices in the courts. Concern about public access to sensitive information is greater in the context of electronic filing because of the risk that the information could be found and spread over the Internet shortly after filing. See, e.g., Minn. Gen. R. Prac. 11 for requirements for submitting restricted identifiers (e.g., social security numbers, etc.) and procedures to address any failure to comply with the requirements. It is not feasible to accept for filing documents that relate to an action pending in another district or to file them in an action under an invalid file number. The acceptance of these documents would only create confusion for the parties, both in the intended district and action and in the district and action where they are mistakenly sent. Similarly, payment of the required filing fee is required by statute, see Minn. Stat. § 357.021, and there is no provision for filing without payment of that required fee. The filing of discovery requests and responses, other than notices of taking depositions, is already prohibited by the second paragraph of this rule; the amended language makes it clear that the court administrators are authorized to reject these unauthorized filings. The rule does not prevent a party from filing an affidavit that incorporates or attaches copies of discovery requests or responses that are authenticated by the affiant.

The rule intentionally omits any recommendation that the absence of a Civil Cover Sheet would result in the rejection of a document for filing. The court can impose an appropriate sanction for this failure after appropriate notice to the parties and, if the court determines it is appropriate, an opportunity to cure the defect. The improper submission of restricted identifiers is addressed in Rule 11.02(3) of these rules and in Rule 11.04 in the General Rules of Practice.

Advisory Committee Comment—2020 Amendments

Rule 5.04(b) is amended to expressly require that proof of service be provided either by: (1) both eFiling and eServing a document together using the court's e-Filing System (with the system-generated proof of service eliminating the need to file separate proof of service); or (2) by filing a separate certificate of service. The amended rule specifies that a certificate of service must be signed under oath or penalty of perjury by the person effecting service. The certificate must also establish the specific time and manner of services, as this information is often required to determine the deadline for response.

Rule 5.04(c) is amended to add the new subdivision (4), to authorize court administrators to reject for filing any document containing restricted identifiers or other information that may not properly be filed in a public document. The specific definitions of what information may not be filed are contained in Rules 11 and 14 of the Minnesota General Rules of Practice for the District Courts.

Rule 5.04(d) is new and is intended to prevent a rejection for filing from having case-ending or other severe consequences for a timely attempt to file a document that contains non-public information. Relief is not automatic under the rule, and in most cases the document will not be deemed filed until a version that complies with the rules is filed. If the filing date is crucial, however, the rule authorizes a motion to have the filing of a compliant version deemed filed as of the time of the original attempted filing. The rule requires that the moving party demonstrate that relief is required "in the interests of justice." This standard does not focus on whether there is a good excuse for the initial, non-compliant document being tendered for filing so much as whether the consequences of rejection are severe or irreparable. This might occur for those relatively rare cases where an action is commenced by filing the complaint. See, e.g., Minn. Stat. § 514.11 (requiring timely filing of mechanic's lien foreclosure action).

5.05. Filing; Facsimile Transmission

Except where filing is required by electronic means by rule of court, any document may be filed with the court by facsimile transmission. Filing shall be deemed complete at the time that the facsimile transmission is received by the court and the filed facsimile shall have the same force and effect as the original. Only facsimile transmission equipment that satisfies the published criteria of the Supreme Court shall be used for filing in accordance with this rule.

Within 7 days after the court has received the transmission, the party filing the document shall forward the following to the court:
 (a) a $25 transmission fee for each 50 pages, or part thereof, of the filing;
 (b) any bulky exhibits or attachments; and
 (c) the applicable filing fee or fees, if any.

If a document is filed by facsimile, the sender's original must not be filed but must be maintained in the files of the party transmitting it for filing and made available to the court or any party to the action upon request.

Upon failure to comply with the requirements of this rule, the court in which the action is pending may make such orders as are just, including but not limited to, an order striking pleadings or parts thereof, staying further proceedings until compliance is complete, or dismissing the action, proceeding, or any part thereof.

(Amended effective January 1, 2020.)

Advisory Committee Comments—2020 Amendments

Rule 5.05 is amended as part of the extensive amendments made to the timing provisions of the rules. These amendments implement the adoption of a standard "day" for counting deadlines under the rules—counting all days regardless of the length of the period and standardizing the time periods, where practicable, to a 7-, 14-, 21- or 28-day schedule.

5.06. Filing Electronically

Where authorized or required by order of the Minnesota Supreme Court or Rule 14 of the General Rules of Practice for the District Courts, documents may, or where required shall, be filed electronically by following the procedures of such order and will be deemed filed in accordance with the provisions of this rule.

A document that is electronically filed is deemed to have been filed by the court administrator on the date and time of its transmittal to the court through the E-Filing System as defined by Rule 14 of the General Rules of Practice for the District Courts, and except for proposed orders, the filing shall be stamped with this date and time if it is subsequently accepted by the court administrator. If the filing is not subsequently accepted by the court administrator

for reasons authorized by Rule 5.04, no date stamp shall be applied and the E-Filing System shall notify the filer that the filing was not accepted.

(Amended effective July 1, 2015.)

Advisory Committee Comment—1993 Amendments

The amendment to Rule 5.04 makes it unnecessary to file notice of taking depositions in the vast majority of cases. Filing may be required as a condition precedent to issuance of a deposition subpoena pursuant to Minn. R. Civ. P. 45.04(a), though that rule only requires proof of service to be shown, not filed, and does not require filing of the notice itself in either event. The notice need not be filed because court administrators should issue subpoenas without the filing of the notice. In practice, courts have little use for deposition notices in court files, and in those rare circumstances where reference to them is necessary, they can be attached as exhibits to an affidavit, filed by leave of court, or offered in evidence just as any other discovery request or response.

Advisory Committee Comments—1996 Amendments

Most of Rule 5.02 is new and for the first time provides for service by facsimile. Service by this method has become widespread, generally handled either by express agreement of counsel or acquiescence in a service method not explicitly authorized by rule.

The committee considered a suggestion that the provision for leaving a document with the court administrator be changed, deleted, or clarified. Although it is not clear from the rule what the administrator should do in the rare event that a document is filed with the administrator rather than delivered or mailed to the attorney, the committee believes the rule should be retained as it provides notice to the court that although service may comply with the rule, effective notice has not been received by the party entitled to notice. This will facilitate the court's consideration of the sufficiency of service under all of the circumstances.

The amendment to Rule 5.02 provides an express mechanism for service by facsimile. Service by facsimile has become widely accepted and is used in Minnesota either by agreement or presumption that it is acceptable under the rules or at least has not been objected to by the parties. The committee believes an express authorization for service by facsimile is appropriate and preferable to the existing silence on the subject. The committee's recommendation is modeled on similar provisions in the Wisconsin and Florida rules. See Wis. Stat. sections 801.14(2) & .15(5)(b); Fla. R. Civ. P. 1.080(b)(5). Service by facsimile is allowed in other jurisdictions as well. See, e.g., Ill. S. Ct. R. 11(b)(4); S. Dak. R. 15-6-5(b); Cal. R. Civ. P. 2008.

In addition providing for service by facsimile, Rule 6.05 is amended to create a specific deadline for timely service. This rule adds an additional day for response to any paper served by any means other than mail (where 3 extra days are allowed under existing Rule 6.05, which is retained) and where service is not effected until after 5:00 p.m., local time. This rule is intended to discourage, or at least make unrewarding, the inappropriate practice of serving papers after the close of a normal business day. Service after 5:00 p.m. is still timely as of the day of service if the deadline for service is that day, but if a response is permitted, the party served has an additional day to respond. This structure parallels directly the mechanism for dealing with service by mail under the existing rule.

Rule 5.05 is amended to add a provision relating to filing that was adopted as part of Fed. R. Civ. P. 5(e) in 1991. It is important that Rule 5 specifically provide that the court administrator must accept for filing documents tendered for that purpose regardless of any technical deficiencies they may contain. The court may, of course, direct that those deficiencies be remedied or give substantive importance to the deficiencies of the documents. The sanction of closing the courthouse to the filing should not be imposed or if imposed, should be imposed by a judge only after reviewing the document and the circumstances surrounding its filing. The rejection of documents for filing may have dire consequences for litigants and is not authorized by statute or rule.

Advisory Committee Comment—2000 Amendments

The last sentence of Rule 5.04 is changed to broaden the direction to court administrators not to reject documents for filing for noncompliance with the form requirements of the rules. The rule as amended makes it clear that those form requirements, regardless of which set of rules contains them, should not be the basis for a refusal to file the document. Any deficiency as to form should be dealt with by appropriate court order, including in most cases an opportunity to cure the defect.

Advisory Committee Comment—2006 Amendments

Rule 5.05 is amended to delete the requirement that an "original" document follow the filing by facsimile. The requirement of a double filing causes confusion and unnecessary burdens for court administrators, and with the dramatic improvement in quality of received faxes since this rule was adopted in 1988, it no longer serves a useful purpose. Under the amended rule, the document filed by facsimile is the original for all purposes unless an issue arises as to its authenticity, in which case the version transmitted electronically and retained by the sender can be reviewed.

The filing fee for fax filings in Rule 5.05 is changed from $5.00 to $25.00 because fax filings, even under the streamlined procedures of the amended rule, still impose significant administrative burdens on court staff, and it is therefore appropriate that this fee, unchanged since the rule's adoption in 1988, be increased. A number of committee members expressed the view that facsimile filing was, and still is, intended to be a process used on a limited basis in exigent or at least unusual circumstances. It is not intended to be a routine filing method.

The rule does not provide a specific mechanism for collecting the transmission fee required under the rule. Because prejudice may occur to a party if a filing is deemed ineffective, the court should determine the appropriate consequences of failure to pay the necessary fee.

Advisory Committee Comment—2010 Amendments

Rule 5.02 is amended to provide for service by electronic means, other than by facsimile as allowed by the existing rule, if authorized by an order of the Minnesota Supreme Court. This amendment is intended to facilitate a pilot project on electronic service and filing in one or two districts, but is designed to be a model for the implementation of electronic filing and service if the pilot project is made permanent and statewide. The rule makes service by electronic means effective when transmission is complete, just as the existing rules provide for filing and service by mail and facsimile transmission.

Service by electronic means is allowed for documents served after the original summons. Service under Rule 4 is required for summonses, and electronic service is not one of the means of service under that rule.

This amendment is modeled on rules 5(b)(2)(D) & (3) of the Federal Rules of Civil Procedure, as amended to implement electronic filing and service in the federal courts.

Rule 5.06 is a new rule to provide for filing by electronic means, if authorized by an order of the Minnesota Supreme Court. This amendment is intended to facilitate a pilot project on electronic service and filing in one or two districts, but is designed to be a model for the implementation of electronic filing if the pilot project is made permanent and statewide. The rule makes filing by electronic means effective in accordance with the rule for the pilot project.

Advisory Committee Comment—2012 Amendment

Rule 5.02 is amended to authorize service by use of an authorized e-filing and e-service system where allowed or required by court rule or supreme court order. This amendment takes effect in conjunction with the adoption of Rule 14 of the General Rules of Practice; that rule defines the cases in which electronic filing and service are either required or permitted, as well as what constitutes proof of service. Rule 5.02(c) addresses the fact of service. Just as service by postal mail is complete upon dropping the properly addressed and postage paid document into the mailbox, service using the court's E-Filing System is complete upon transmitting the electronic document to the E-Filing system using the appropriate service command. Rule 5.02(d) provides specific guidance for courts dealing with the rare, but probably inevitable, circumstance of the e-filing system either not being available or not functioning as intended. If applicable, the rule authorizes the court to deem pleadings served or filed (or both) when attempted and to adjust the time to respond as appropriate.

Rule 5.04 is amended to specify the limited situations where courts are not required to accept documents tendered for filing. These situations apply equally to documents tendered for filing electronically, by mail, or by hand-delivery to the court. Rejection for filing is not required in each of these situations, and it may be possible that certain format defects might be "fixed" at the time of filing. For example, if an incorrect file number is used on a document and it is detected at the time of attempted filing, it might be corrected; the administrator is still authorized to reject it for filing. An attempt to file a case using a new case number when the case has previously been filed may also be treated as not having the correct file number.

Rule 5.05 is amended to dovetail the facsimile filing and service provisions to mandatory use of e-filing and e-service in certain cases. Where the court rules require e-filing and e-service, filing and service by facsimile are not authorized. When e-filing and e-service are in use throughout the state and in all categories of cases, facsimile filing and service is likely to become unavailable.

Rule 5.06 is amended to clarify when electronic filing through the court's e-filing system is effective. E-filings are subject to acceptance by the court administrator and acceptance may or may not occur on the same day as the transmittal of the filing. If accepted by the court administrator, however, the e-filing party will get the benefit of the date and time of their transmittal as the effective date of their filing.

Advisory Committee Comments—2015 Amendments

This rule incorporates the provisions of Minn. Gen. R. Prac. 14 on the operation of electronic filing and the determination of the date of filing where it is accomplished by use of the court's E-Filing System.

The use of the alternative "may or shall" language in the first paragraph reflects the expectation that the implementation of electronic filing and service is likely to involve some period of time where e-filing and e-service may be required for some actions (based on district, county, or type of actions), permitted for others, or not permitted at all. The rules are designed to implement e-filing and e-service in particular actions as established by separate implementation orders.

RULE 5A. NOTICE OF CONSTITUTIONAL CHALLENGE TO A STATUTE

A party that files a pleading, written motion, or other document drawing into question the constitutionality of a federal or state statute must promptly:
- (1) file a notice of constitutional question stating the question and identifying the document that raises it, if:
    - (A) a federal statute is questioned and neither the United States nor any of its agencies, officers, or employees is a party in an official capacity, or

(B) a state statute is questioned and neither the state nor any of its agencies, officers, or employees is a party in an official capacity; and

(2) serve the notice and document on the Attorney General of the United States if a federal statute is challenged, or on the Minnesota Attorney General if a state statute is challenged, by United States Mail to afford the Attorney General an opportunity to intervene.

(Amended effective July 1, 2015.)

Advisory Committee Comment—2007 Amendment

Rule 5A is a new rule, though it addresses subject matter covered by Minn. R. Civ. P. 24.04 prior to the adoption of this rule. The rule imposes an express requirement for notice to the appropriate Attorney General—the Minnesota Attorney General for challenges to Minnesota statutes and the Attorney General of the United States for challenges to federal statutes. The rule requires the giving of notice, and the purpose of the notice is to permit the Attorney General receiving it to decide whether to intervene in the action. The rule does not require any action by the Attorney General and in many instances intervention will not be sought until the litigation reaches the appellate courts. The federal rule requires service on the appropriate attorney general by certified or registered mail. The committee believes that service of this notice by U.S. Mail is sufficient for this purpose.

As part of this change, Minn. R. Civ. P. 24.04 is abrogated as it duplicates this rule's mechanism.

RULE 6. TIME

6.01. Computation

(a) Computing Time. The following rules apply in computing any time period specified in these rules, in any local rule or court order, or in any statute that does not specify a method of computing time.

(1) Period Stated in Days or a Longer Unit of Time. When the period is stated in days or a longer unit of time:
   (A) exclude the day of the event that triggers the period;
   (B) count every day, including intermediate Saturdays, Sundays, and legal holidays; and
   (C) include the last day of the period, but if the last day is a Saturday, Sunday, or legal holiday, the period continues to run until the end of the next day that is not a Saturday, Sunday, or legal holiday.
(2) Periods Shorter than 7 Days. Only if expressly so provided by any other rule or statute, a time period that is less than 7 days may exclude intermediate Saturdays, Sundays, and legal holidays.
(3) Period Stated in Hours. When the period is stated in hours:
   (A) begin counting immediately on the occurrence of the event that triggers the period;

(B) count every hour, including hours occurring during intermediate Saturdays, Sundays, and legal holidays; and

(C) if the period would end on a Saturday, Sunday, or legal holiday, the period continues to run until the same time on the next day that is not a Saturday, Sunday, or legal holiday.

(4) Inaccessibility of the Court Administrator's Office. Unless the court orders otherwise, if the court administrator's office is inaccessible:

(A) on the last day for filing or service under Rule 6.01(a)(1), then the time for filing is extended to the first accessible day that is not a Saturday, Sunday, or legal holiday; or

(B) during the last hour for filing under Rule 6.01(a)(1), then the time for filing is extended to the same time on the first accessible day that is not a Saturday, Sunday, or legal holiday.

(b) "Last Day" Defined. Unless a different time is set by a statute, local rule, or court order, the last day ends:

(1) for electronic filing, at 11:59 p.m. local Minnesota time; and

(2) for filing by other means, when the Court Administrator's office is scheduled to close.

(c) "Next Day" Defined. The "next day" is determined by continuing to count forward when the period is measured after an event and backward when measured before an event.

(d) **Definition of Legal Holiday.** As used in this rule and in Rule 77(c), "legal holiday" includes any holiday designated in Minn. Stat. § 645.44, subd. 5, as a holiday for the state or any state-wide branch of government and any day that the United States Mail does not operate.

(e) Additional Time After Service by Mail or Service Late in Day. Whenever a party has the right or is required to do some act or take some proceedings within a prescribed period after the service of a notice or other document upon the party, and the notice or document is served upon the party by United States Mail, 3 days shall be added to the prescribed period.

If service is made by any means other than United States Mail and accomplished after 5:00 p.m. local Minnesota time on the day of service, 1 additional day shall be added to the prescribed period.

(Amended effective January 1, 2020.)

6.02. Enlargement

When by statute, by these rules, by a notice given thereunder, or by order of court an act is required or allowed to be done at or within a specified time, the court for cause shown may, at any time in its discretion, (1) with or without motion or notice order the period enlarged if request therefor is made before the expiration of the period originally prescribed or as extended by a previous order, or (2) upon motion made after the expiration of the specified period permit the act to be done where the failure to act was the result of excusable neglect; but it may not extend the time for taking any action under Rules 4.043, 59.03, 59.05, and 60.02 except to the extent and under the conditions stated in them.

6.03. Unaffected by Expiration of Term

The continued existence or the expiration of a term of court does not affect or limit the period of time provided for the taking of any action or proceeding, or affect the power of the court to act or take any proceeding in any action which has been pending before it.

6.04. For Motions; Affidavits

The deadlines for service and filing of motions, as well as affidavits and other documents in support of responding to motions, are governed by the Minnesota General Rules of Practice.

(Amended effective January 1, 2020.)

6.05 [Abrogated]

Advisory Committee Comments--1996 Amendments

The amendment to Rule 6.01 conforms the rule to its federal counterpart. The committee believes it is desirable to define explicitly what constitutes a "legal holiday." Given the nature of Minnesota's weather, the committee believes specific provision for dealing with inclement weather should be made in the rules. The federal rule enumerates specific holidays. That drafting approach is not feasible in Minnesota because Minnesota Statutes, section 645.44, subdivision 5, defines legal holidays, but allows the judiciary to pick either Columbus Day or the Friday after Thanksgiving as a holiday. Whichever is selected is defined to be a holiday under the rule.

The amendment to Rule 6.05 conforms the rule to the federal rule except for the last sentence which is new and has no federal counterpart. This provision is intended to discourage the unseemly practices of sliding a "service" under the door of opposing counsel or sending a facsimile transmission after the close of business and asserting timely service. Such service will be timely under the rules, but will add a day to the time to respond. If the paper is due to be served a fixed number of days before an event, that number should be increased by one as well, making it necessary to serve late in the day before the deadline.

Advisory Committee Comment—2007 Amendment

Rule 6.01 is amended to remove potential ambiguity in the existing rule. The rule is ambiguous because of the odd definition of "holiday" in MINN. STAT. § 645.44, subd. 5, and its ambiguity over how Columbus Day is treated. Additionally, because the rules explicitly provide for service by mail, the court recognized that a "mail holiday" should be a "legal holiday" for the purpose of this rule.

The rule excuses filing on the last day of a time period if the court administrator's office is inaccessible. The amended rule replaces an indefinite concept of the court administrator's office being "inaccessible" with a more definite formulation: the office of the administrator of the court where the action is pending must actually be closed.

Rule 6.05 is amended to make the rule definite as to what forms of service qualify as "service by mail." The rule as amended explicitly allows three additional days only for service by United States Mail; the use of any other delivery or courier service does not constitute "United States Mail," and therefore does not qualify for additional time. This rule is now consistent with Minn. R. Civ. P. 4.05, which specifies "first-class mail" as the means for service by mail.

Advisory Committee Comment—2012 Amendment

Rule 6.01 is amended to add unavailability of the court-authorized e-filing and e-service system as a circumstance that would result in the extension of the time period. This extension applies only where the system problem occurs on the last day of the period and should only apply where the problem is not momentary. The rule requires that unavailability of the e-filing system actually prevent compliance with the service or filing requirements. This certainly eliminates use of a short-lived shutdown from extending the deadline except, possibly, where it occurs right at the end of the day. Where the shutdown occurs for a substantial part of the day and where it continues through the close of business, then the additional day would be automatically applied.

Advisory Committee Comment—2015 Amendment

Rule 6.05 is amended to remove a potential ambiguity in the existing rule—the 5:00 p.m. deadline for service is to be accomplished without allowing an additional day for response is defined to be Minnesota time. This provision will be especially important for service using the court's E-Filing System, by which service could be effected from anywhere in the world.

Advisory Committee Comment—2020 Amendment

The amendments to Rule 6.01 are important and are the key to the amendments to several other rules relating to timing. These amendments implement the adoption of a standard "day" for counting deadlines under the rules—counting all days regardless of the length of the period and standardizing the time periods, where practicable, to a 7-, 14-, 21- or 28-day schedule. The most important change is found in Rule 6.01(a)(1)(B), which establishes "a day is a day"—all days during a period under the rules, regardless of length, are included, including weekends and legal holidays. This change mirrors a set of changes made in the Federal Rules of Civil Procedure, and is intended to create substantial similarity between "state days" and "federal days." Minnesota and the federal government recognize slightly different legal holidays.
Rule 4.06 has for years required that proof of service include the time of service for all forms of service other than service by publication. Compliance with Rule 4.06 is especially important because of the need to know the time of service in order to calculate response deadlines.
Rule 6.01(c) is also an important provision that will affect many deadlines. It establishes an explicit rule for how days are counted when counting "backwards" from a deadline. The rule requires that, when counting backwards from an event, and the last day falls on a weekend or holiday, the counting continues to the next earlier date that is not a weekend or holiday. This rule is modeled on its federal counterpart and is intended to create greater uniformity in timing between state and federal court matters.
Rule 6.01(e) appears as new text, but is the former Rule 6.05 relocated to Rule 6.01 because it addresses the same timing matters.

Rule 6.04 is rewritten because it is superseded by the more specific provisions of Rule 115 of the Minnesota General Rules of Practice. Additionally, Rule 56 of the civil rules establishes a very important deadline for summary judgment motions—"in no event shall the motion be served less than 14 days before the time fixed for the hearing." Minn. R. Civ. P. 56.02. This limit on shortened notice recognizes the power of the summary judgment motion and its potential to be case or defense-terminating and provides an opportunity for the responding party to prepare a response and be heard.

Rule 6.05 is abrogated only because its text is now incorporated in Rule 6.01(e).

III. PLEADINGS AND MOTIONS

RULE 7. PLEADINGS ALLOWED; FORM OF MOTIONS

7.01. Pleadings

There shall be a complaint and an answer (including such pleadings in a third-party proceeding when a third-party claim is asserted); a reply to a counterclaim denominated as such; and an answer to a cross-claim if the answer contains a cross-claim. No other pleading shall be allowed except that the court may order a reply to an answer. Demurrers, pleas and exceptions for insufficiency of a pleading shall not be used.

7.02. Motions and Other Documents

(a) An application to the court for an order shall be by motion which, unless made during a hearing or trial, shall be in writing, shall state with particularity the grounds therefor, and shall set forth the relief or order sought. The requirement of writing is fulfilled if the motion is stated in a written notice of the hearing of the motion. Motions provided in these rules are motions requiring a written notice to the party and a hearing before the order can be issued unless the particular rule under which the motion is made specifically provides that the motion may be made ex parte. The parties may agree to written submission to the court for decision without oral argument unless the court directs otherwise. Upon the request of a party or upon its own initiative, the court may hear any motion by telephone conference.

(b) The rules applicable for captions, signing, and other matters of form of pleadings apply to all motions and other documents provided for by these rules.

(c) All motions will be signed in accordance with Rule 11.

(Amended effective July 1, 2015.)

RULE 8. GENERAL RULES OF PLEADING

8.01. Claims for Relief

A pleading which sets forth a claim for relief, whether an original claim, counterclaim, cross-claim, or third-party claim, shall contain a short and plain statement of the claim showing that the pleader is entitled to relief and a demand for judgment for the relief sought; if a recovery of money is demanded, the amount shall be stated. Relief in the alternative or of several different types may be demanded. If a recovery of money for unliquidated damages is demanded in an amount less than $50,000, the amount shall be stated. If a recovery of money for unliquidated damages in an amount greater than $50,000 is demanded, the pleading shall state merely that recovery of reasonable damages in an amount greater than $50,000 is sought.

8.02. Defenses; Form of Denials

A party shall state in short and plain terms any defenses to each claim asserted and shall admit or deny the averments upon which the adverse party relies. If a party is without knowledge or information sufficient to form a belief as to the truth of an averment, the party shall so state and this has the effect of a denial. Denials shall fairly meet the substance of the averments denied. A pleader who intends in good faith to deny only a part or to qualify an averment shall specify so much of it as is true and material and shall deny only the remainder. Unless the pleader intends in good faith to controvert all the averments of the preceding pleading, the pleader may make denials as specific denials of designated averments or paragraphs, or may generally deny all the averments except such designated averments or paragraphs as the pleader expressly admits. However, a pleader who intends to controvert all its averments may do so by general denial subject to the obligations set forth in Rule 11.

8.03. Affirmative Defenses

In pleading to a preceding pleading, a party shall set forth affirmatively accord and satisfaction, arbitration and award, assumption of risk, contributory negligence, discharge in bankruptcy, duress, estoppel, failure of consideration, fraud, illegality, injury by fellow servant, laches, license, payment, release, res judicata, statute of frauds, statute of limitations, waiver, and any other matter constituting an avoidance or affirmative defense. When a party has mistakenly designated a defense as a counterclaim or a counterclaim as a defense, the court, on such terms as justice may require, shall treat the pleading as if there had been a proper designation.

8.04. Effect of Failure to Deny

Averments in a pleading to which a responsive pleading is required, other than those as to amount of damage, are admitted when not denied in the responsive pleading. Averments in a pleading to which no responsive pleading is required or permitted shall be taken as denied or avoided.

8.05. Pleading to be Concise and Direct; Consistency

(a) Each averment of a pleading shall be simple, concise, and direct. No technical forms of pleading or motions are required.

(b) A party may set forth two or more statements of a claim or defense alternatively or hypothetically, either in one count or defense or in separate counts or defenses. When two or more statements are made in the alternative and one of them if made independently would be sufficient, the pleading is not made insufficient by the insufficiency of one or more of the alternative statements. A party may also state as many separate claims or defenses as the party has regardless of consistency and whether based on legal or equitable grounds or both. All statements shall be made subject to the obligations set forth in Rule 11.

8.06. Construction of Pleadings

All pleadings shall be so construed as to do substantial justice.

RULE 9. PLEADING SPECIAL MATTERS

9.01. Capacity

It is not necessary to aver the capacity of a party to sue or be sued, the authority of a party to sue or be sued in a representative capacity, or the legal existence of a partnership or an organized association of persons that is made a party. A party who desires to raise an issue as to the legal existence of any party, the capacity of any party to sue or be sued, or the authority of a party to sue or be sued in a representative capacity shall do so by specific negative averment, which shall include such supporting particulars as are peculiarly within the pleader's knowledge.

9.02. Fraud, Mistake, Condition of Mind

In all averments of fraud or mistake, the circumstances constituting fraud or mistake shall be stated with particularity. Malice, intent, knowledge, and other condition of mind of a person may be averred generally.

9.03. Conditions Precedent

In pleading the performance or occurrence of conditions precedent, it is sufficient to aver generally that all conditions precedent have been performed or have occurred. A denial of performance or occurrence shall be made specifically and with particularity.

9.04. Official Document or Act

In pleading an official document or official act, it is sufficient to aver that the document was issued or the act was done in compliance with law; and in pleading any ordinance of a city, village, or borough or any special or local statute or any right derived from either, it is sufficient to refer to the ordinance or statute by its title and the date of its approval.

9.05. Judgment

In pleading a judgment or decision of a domestic or foreign court, judicial or quasi-judicial tribunal, or of a board or officer, it is sufficient to aver the judgment or decision without setting forth matter showing jurisdiction to render it.

9.06. Time and Place

For the purpose of testing the sufficiency of a pleading, averments of time and place are material and shall be considered like all other averments of material matter.

9.07. Special Damages

When items of special damage are claimed, they shall be specifically stated.

9.08. Unknown Party; How Designated

When a party is ignorant of the name of an opposing party and so alleges in the party's pleading, the opposing party may be designated by any name and when that opposing party's true name is discovered the process and all pleadings and proceedings in the action may be amended by substituting the true name.

RULE 10. FORM OF PLEADINGS

10.01. Caption; Names of Parties

Every pleading shall have a caption setting forth the name of the court and the county in which the action is brought, the title of the action, the court file number if one has been assigned, and a designation as in Rule 7, and, in the upper right-hand corner, the appropriate case type as set forth in the Case Type Index as published by the State Court Administration and maintained on the state court website (www.mncourts.gov). If a case is assigned to a particular judge for all subsequent proceedings, the name of that judge shall be included in the caption and adjacent to the file number. In the complaint, the title of the action shall include the names of all the parties, but in other pleadings it is sufficient to state the first party on each side with an appropriate indication of other parties. A party may be identified by initials or pseudonym only where authorized by law or court order.

(Amended effective July 1, 2018.)

Advisory Committee Comments - 2000 Amendments

Rule 10.01 is amended to facilitate case management and document management in cases where a judge has been assigned to the case. By placing the judge's name on the caption, it is often possible to expedite the delivery of filed documents to that judge. This provision is commonly required in federal court cases where all matters are assigned to a judge, including in the United States District Court for the District of Minnesota. See LR 5.1 (D. Minn.). The rule is also amended to require the inclusion of a court file number if one has been assigned.

Advisory Committee Comments - 2017 Amendments

Rule 10.01 is amended to move the list of required case types from Form 23 in the Appendix of Forms and to replace it with a Case Type Index to be maintained and available on the state court website. Case types have evolved over time, and this change will both bring the list up to date and provide a mechanism for it to be modified in the future without additional court orders. The case types on the Case type Index should match those provided by drop-down menus in the district courts' e-filing system.

Advisory Committee Comment—2018 Amendments

Rule 10.01 is amended to add the final sentence to clarify that, although actions must normally be brought in the name of the real party in interest (see Rule 17.01), in certain limited circumstances the court may allow a party to proceed anonymously. In actions brought pursuant to Minn. Stat. § 604.31 for the nonconsensual dissemination of private sexual images (so-called "revenge porn"), the party is entitled to an order allowing anonymity (such as by using the pseudonym "John Doe" or "Jane Doe" or a party's real or substituted initials), but a court order is still required. In other exceptional circumstances, a party must obtain leave of court to proceed either under a pseudonym or by initials, and that relief is governed by the court's discretion.

10.02. Paragraph; Separate Statements

All averments of claim or defense shall be made in numbered paragraphs, the contents of each of which shall be limited as far as practicable to a statement of a single set of circumstances; and a paragraph may be referred to by number in all succeeding pleadings. Each claim founded upon a separate transaction or occurrence and each defense other than denials shall be stated in a separate count or defense whenever a separation facilitates the clear presentation of the matters set forth.

10.03. Adoption by Reference; Exhibits

Statements in a pleading may be adopted by reference in a different part of the same pleading or in another pleading or in any motion. A copy of any written instrument which is an exhibit to a pleading is a part of the statement of claim or defense set forth in the pleading.

10.04. Failure to Comply

If a pleading, motion or other document fails to indicate the case type as required by Rule 10.01, it may be stricken by the court unless the appropriate case type indicator is communicated to the court administrator promptly after the omission is called to the attention of the pleader or movant.

(Amended effective July 1, 2015.)

RULE 11. SIGNING OF PLEADINGS, MOTIONS, AND OTHER DOCUMENTS; REPRESENTATIONS TO COURT; SANCTIONS

11.01. Signature

Every pleading, written motion, and other similar document shall be signed by at least one attorney of record in the attorney's individual name, or, if the party is self-represented, shall be signed by the party. Each document shall state the signer's address and telephone number and e-mail address, if any, and attorney registration number if signed by an attorney. Except when otherwise specifically provided by rule or statute, pleadings need not be verified or accompanied by affidavit. An unsigned document shall be stricken unless omission of the signature is corrected promptly after being called to the attention of the attorney or party. If authorized by order of the Minnesota Supreme Court or by rule of court, a document filed, signed, or verified by electronic means in accordance with that order constitutes a signed document for the purposes of applying these rules.

The filing or submitting of a document using an E-Filing System established by rule of court constitutes certification of compliance with the signature requirements of the applicable court rules.

(Amended effective July 1, 2015.)

11.02. Representations to Court

By presenting to the court (whether by signing, filing, submitting, or later advocating) a pleading, written motion, or other document, an attorney or self-represented litigant is certifying that to the best of the person's knowledge, information, and belief, formed after an inquiry reasonable under the circumstances;

(a) it is not being presented for any improper purpose, such as to harass or to cause unnecessary delay or needless increase in the cost of litigation;

(b) the claims, defenses, and other legal contentions therein are warranted by existing law or by a nonfrivolous argument for the extension, modification, or reversal of existing law or the establishment of new law;

(c) the allegations and other factual contentions have evidentiary support or, if specifically so identified, are likely to have evidentiary support after a reasonable opportunity for further investigation or discovery;

(d) the denials of factual contentions are warranted on the evidence or, if specifically so identified, are reasonably based on a lack of information or belief; and

(e) the pleading, motion, or other document does not include any restricted identifiers and that all restricted identifiers have been submitted in a confidential manner as required by Rule 11 of the General Rules of Practice for the District Courts. Notwithstanding Rule 11.03(a)(1) of these rules, a party shall not be required to wait 21 days before filing or presenting a motion seeking relief from the court in regard to the proper submission of documents containing restricted identifiers.

(Amended effective July 1, 2015.)

11.03. Sanctions

If, after notice and a reasonable opportunity to respond, the court determines that Rule 11.02 of these rules has been violated, the court may, subject to the conditions stated below, impose an appropriate sanction upon the attorneys, law firms, or parties that have violated Rule 11.02 or are responsible for the violation. This rule does not limit the imposition of sanctions authorized by other rules, statutes, or the inherent power of the court.

(a) **How Initiated.**

(1) By Motion. A motion for sanctions under this rule shall be made separately from other motions or requests and shall describe the specific conduct alleged to violate Rule 11.02. It shall be served as provided in Rule 5, but shall not be filed with or presented to the court unless, within 21 days after service of the motion (or such other period as the court may prescribe), the challenged document, claim, defense, contention, allegation, or denial is not withdrawn or appropriately corrected. If warranted, the court may award to the party prevailing on the motion the reasonable expenses and attorney fees incurred in presenting or opposing the motion. Absent exceptional circumstances, a law firm shall be held jointly responsible for violations committed by its partners, associates, and employees.

(2) On Court's Initiative. On its own initiative, the court may enter an order describing the specific conduct that appears to violate Rule 11.02 and directing an attorney, law firm, or party to show cause why it has not violated Rule 11.02 with respect thereto.

(b) **Nature of Sanction; Limitations.** A sanction imposed for violation of this rule shall be limited to what is sufficient to deter repetition of such conduct or comparable conduct by others similarly situated. Subject to the limitations in Rules 11.03(a)(1) and (2), the sanction may consist of, or include, directives of a nonmonetary nature, an order to pay a penalty into court, or, if imposed on motion and warranted for effective deterrence, an order directing payment to the movant of some or all of the reasonable attorney fees and other expenses incurred as a direct result of the violation.

(1) Monetary sanctions may not be awarded against a represented party for a violation of Rule 11.02 (b).

(2) Monetary sanctions may not be awarded on the court's initiative unless the court issues its order to show cause before a voluntary dismissal or settlement of the claims made by or against the party which is, or whose attorneys are, to be sanctioned.

(c) **Order.** When imposing sanctions, the court shall describe the conduct determined to constitute a violation of this rule and explain the basis for the sanction imposed.

(Amended effective July 1, 2015.)

11.04. Inapplicability to Discovery

Rules 11.01-.03 do not apply to discovery requests, responses, objections, and motions that are subject to the provisions of Rules 26 through 37.

(Amended effective August 1, 2000.)

Task Force Comment--1991 Adoption

This rule amendment is patterned after 4th Dist. R. 1.01(c) & (e).

The Task Force believes that the simple additional requirement for signing pleadings, widely followed in practice, should best be made part of this rule governing signing of pleadings, motions and other papers.

Advisory Committee Comments--2000 Amendments

Rule 11 is amended to conform completely to the federal rule. While Rule 11 has worked fairly well in its current form under the Supreme Court's guidance in Uselman v. Uselman, 464 N.W.2d 130 (Minn. 1990), the federal rules have been amended and create both procedural and substantive differences between state and federal court practices. Additionally, the Minnesota Legislature has created a statutory mechanism that follows the federal procedure, resulting in a confusing array of practice requirements and remedies. See Minnesota Statutes, section 549.211. On balance, the Committee believes that the amendment of the Rule to conform to its federal counterpart makes the most sense, given this Committee's long-standing preference for minimizing the differences between state and federal practice unless compelling local interests or long-entrenched reliance on the state procedure makes changing a rule inappropriate.

It is the intention of the Committee that the revised Rule would modify the procedure for seeking sanctions, but would not significantly change the availability of sanctions or the conduct justifying the imposition of sanctions. Courts and practitioners should be guided by the Uselman decision, cited above, and should continue to reserve the seeking of sanctions and their imposition for substantial departures from acceptable litigation conduct.

Advisory Committee Comment—2010 Amendment

Rule 11.01 is amended to add the last sentence. This amendment makes it clear that "signing" in accordance with a rule allowing for filing and service by electronic means where authorized by an order of the Minnesota Supreme Court is treated as a signature for the purpose of Rule 11 or other provision in the rules. This amendment is intended to facilitate a pilot project on electronic filing in one or two districts, but is designed to be a model for the implementation of electronic filing and service if the pilot project is made permanent and statewide.

Advisory Committee Comment—2012 Amendment

Rule 11.01 is amended to add the second paragraph. The sole purpose of the amendment is to make explicit the status of "signatures" affixed to pleadings and other documents that are electronically served. Whatever means is used to sign these documents, whether quill pen and ink, facsimile of a signature, or an indication that the document is signed (such as a "/s/ Pat Smith" notation), each will be treated the same way and deemed to be signatures for all purposes under the rule.

Advisory Committee Comments—2015 Amendments

The only substantive amendment to Rule 11 is found in Rule 11.02, which adds an additional certification made upon the signing of a pleading. Under this provision, signing a pleading is deemed to be a certification that the pleading does not contain any restricted identifiers in violation of Rule 11 of the General Rules of Practice. Rule 11.03 is amended in 2015 to recognize that relief is available under other rules including Gen. R. Prac. 11.04 regarding improper submission of restricted identifiers.

The remaining amendments to Rule 11 are not substantive in nature or intended effect. The replacement of "paper" with "document" is made through these rules, and simply advances precision in choice of language. Most documents will not be filed as "paper" documents, so paper is retired as a descriptor of them.

"Self-represented litigant" is used uniformly throughout the judicial branch, and is preferable to "non-represented party" and "pro se party," both to avoid a Latin phrase not used outside legal jargon and because it facilitates the drafting of clearer rules.

RULE 12. DEFENSES AND OBJECTIONS; WHEN AND HOW PRESENTED; BY PLEADING OR MOTION; MOTION FOR JUDGMENT ON PLEADINGS

12.01. When Presented

Defendant shall serve an answer within 21 days after service of the summons upon that defendant unless the court directs otherwise pursuant to Rule 4.043. A party served with a pleading stating a cross-claim against that party shall serve an answer thereto within 21 days after the service upon that party. The plaintiff shall serve a reply to a counterclaim in the answer within 21 days after service of the answer or, if a reply is ordered by the court, within 21 days after service of the order, unless the order otherwise directs. The service of a motion permitted under this rule alters these periods of time as follows unless a different time is fixed by order of the court: (1) If the court denies the motion or postpones its disposition until the trial on the merits, the responsive pleading shall be served within 14 days after service of notice of the court's action; (2) if the court grants a motion for a more definite statement, the responsive pleading shall be served within 14 days after the service of the more definite statement.

(Amended effective January 1, 2020.)

Advisory Committee Comment—2018 Amendments

Rule 12.01 establishes the time to respond to a complaint. In 2017 the Minnesota Legislature adopted a statute that extends the time to respond to certain actions relating to architectural barriers to public access to buildings. See Minn. Laws 2017, ch. 80, §§ 7 & 3, to be codified as Minn. Stat. § 363A.331, subds. 2 & 2a. The statute applies to actions brought on or after May 24, 2017.

12.02. How Presented

Every defense, in law or fact, to a claim for relief in any pleading, whether a claim, counterclaim, cross-claim, or third-party claim, shall be asserted in the responsive pleading thereto if one is required, except that the following defenses may at the option of the pleader be made by motion:

(a) lack of jurisdiction over the subject matter;
(b) lack of jurisdiction over the person;
(c) insufficiency of process;
(d) insufficiency of service of process;
(e) failure to state a claim upon which relief can be granted; and
(f) failure to join a party pursuant to Rule 19.

A motion making any of these defenses shall be made before pleading if a further pleading is permitted. No defense or objection is waived by being joined with one or more defenses or objections in a responsive pleading or motion. If a pleading sets forth a claim for relief to which the adverse party is not required to serve a responsive pleading, the adverse party may assert at the trial any defense in law or fact to that claim for relief. If, on a motion asserting the defense that the pleading fails to state a claim upon which relief can be granted, matters outside the pleading are presented to and not excluded by the court, the motion shall be treated as one for summary judgment and disposed of as provided in Rule 56, and all parties shall be given reasonable opportunity to present all material made pertinent to such a motion by Rule 56.

12.03. Motion for Judgment on the Pleadings

After the pleadings are closed but within such time as not to delay the trial, any party may move for judgment on the pleadings. If, on such motion, matters outside the pleadings are presented to and not excluded by the court, the motion shall be treated as one for summary judgment and disposed of as provided for in Rule 56, and all parties shall be given reasonable opportunity to present all material made pertinent to such a motion by Rule 56.

(Amended effective March 1, 1994.)

Advisory Committee Comment--1993 Amendments

The only change made to this rule is to correct a typographical or grammatical error in the existing rule. No change in meaning or interpretation is intended.

12.04. Preliminary Hearing

The defenses and relief enumerated in Rules 12.02 and 12.03, whether made in a pleading or by motion, shall be heard and determined before trial on application of any party unless the court orders that the hearing and determination thereof be deferred until the trial.

12.05. Motion for More Definite Statement, for Paragraphing and for Separate Statement

If a pleading to which a responsive pleading is permitted violates the provisions of Rule 10.02, or is so vague and ambiguous that a party cannot reasonably be required to frame a responsive pleading, the party may move for a compliance with Rule 10.02 or for a more definite statement before interposing a responsive pleading. The motion shall point out the defects complained of and the details desired. If the motion is granted and the order of the court is not obeyed within 14 days after service of notice of the order or within such other time as the court may fix, the court may strike the pleading to which the motion was directed or make such order as it deems just.

(Amended effective January 1, 2020.)

12.06. Motion to Strike

Upon motion made by a party before responding to a pleading or, if no responsive pleading is permitted by these rules, upon motion made by a party within 21 days after the service of the pleading upon the party, or upon its own initiative at any time, the court may order any pleading not in compliance with Rule 11 stricken as sham and false, or may order stricken from any pleading any insufficient defense or any redundant, immaterial, impertinent or scandalous matter.

(Amended effective January 1, 2020.)

12.07. Consolidation of Defenses in Motion

A party who makes a motion pursuant to this rule may join with it other motions then available to the party. If a party makes a motion under this rule but omits therefrom any then available defense or objection which this rule permits to be raised by motion, that party shall not thereafter make a motion based on the defense or objection so omitted, except a motion as provided in Rule 12.08(b) hereof on any of the grounds there stated.

12.08. Waiver or Preservation of Certain Defenses

(a) A defense of lack of jurisdiction over the person, insufficiency of process, or insufficiency of service of process is waived (1) if omitted from a motion in the circumstances described in Rule 12.07, or (2) if it is neither made by motion pursuant to this rule nor included in a responsive pleading or an amendment thereof permitted by Rule 15.01 to be made as a matter of course.

(b) A defense of failure to state a claim upon which relief can be granted, a defense of failure to join a party indispensable under Rule 19, and an objection of failure to state a legal defense to a claim may be made in any pleading permitted or ordered pursuant to Rule 7.01, or by motion for judgment on the pleadings, or at the trial on the merits.

(c) Whenever it appears by suggestion of the parties or otherwise that the court lacks jurisdiction of the subject matter, the court shall dismiss the action.

Advisory Committee Comment—2020 Amendments

Rule 12.01 is amended as part of the amendments made to the timing provisions of the rules. These amendments implement the adoption of a standard "day" for counting deadlines under the rules—counting all days regardless of the length of the period and standardizing the time periods, where practicable, to a 7-, 14-, 21- or 28-day schedule. The changes to this rule change only the time limits, and are not intended to have any other effect.

Rule 12.05 is amended as part of the amendments made to the timing provisions of the rules. These amendments implement the adoption of a standard "day" for counting deadlines under the rules—counting all days regardless of the length of the period and standardizing the time periods, where practicable, to a 7-, 14-, 21- or 28-day schedule. The only change to this rule lengthens the 10-day period to respond to an order under the rule to 14 days. This changes only the time limit, and is not intended to have any other effect.

Rule 12.06 is amended as part of the amendments made to the timing provisions of the rules. These amendments implement the adoption of a standard "day" for counting deadlines under the rules—counting all days regardless of the length of the period and standardizing the time periods, where practicable, to a 7-, 14-, 21- or 28-day schedule. The only change to this rule lengthens the 20-day period to file a motion to strike to 21 days. This changes only the time limit to make it consistent with the deadline to answer contained in Rule 12.01, and is not intended to have any other effect.

RULE 13. COUNTERCLAIM AND CROSS-CLAIM

13.01. Compulsory Counterclaims

A pleading shall state as a counterclaim any claim which at the time of serving the pleading the pleader has against any opposing party, if it arises out of the transaction that is the subject matter of the opposing party's claim and does not require for its adjudication the presence of third parties over whom the court cannot acquire jurisdiction, except that such a claim need not be so stated if, at the time the action was commenced, the claim was the subject of another pending action.

13.02. Permissive Counterclaims

A pleading may state as a counterclaim any claim against an opposing party not arising out of the transaction that is the subject matter of the opposing party's claim.

13.03. Counterclaim Exceeding Opposing Claim

A counterclaim may or may not diminish or defeat the recovery sought by the opposing party. It may claim relief exceeding in amount or different in kind from that sought in the pleading of the opposing party.

13.04. Counterclaim Against the State of Minnesota

These rules shall not be construed to enlarge beyond the limits now fixed by law the right to assert counterclaims or to claim credits against the State of Minnesota or an officer or agency thereof.

13.05. Counterclaim Maturing or Acquired After Pleading

A claim which either matured or was acquired by the pleader after serving a pleading may, by leave of court, be presented as a counterclaim by supplemental pleading.

13.06. Omitted Counterclaim

When a pleader fails to set up a counterclaim through oversight, inadvertence, or excusable neglect, or when justice requires, the pleader may, by leave of court, set up the counterclaim by amendment.

13.07. Cross-Claim Against Co-Party

A pleading may state as a cross-claim any claim by one party against a co-party arising out of the transaction or occurrence that is the subject matter either of the original action or of a counterclaim therein or relating to any property that is the subject matter of the original action. Such cross-claim may include a claim that the party against whom it is asserted is or may be liable to the cross-claimant for all or part of a claim asserted in the action against the cross-claimant.

13.08. Joinder of Additional Parties

Persons other than those made parties to the original action may be made parties to a counterclaim or cross-claim in accordance with the provisions of Rules 19 and 20.

13.09. Separate Trials; Separate Judgment

If the court orders separate trials as provided in Rule 42.02, judgment on a counterclaim or cross-claim may be rendered in accordance with the terms of Rule 54.02 even if the claims of the opposing party have been dismissed or disposed of otherwise.

RULE 14. THIRD-PARTY PRACTICE

14.01. When a Defending Party May Bring in a Third Party
    (a) Timing of the Summons and Complaint. A defending party may, as third-party plaintiff, serve a summons and complaint on a nonparty who is or may be liable to it for all or part of the claim against it. But the third-party plaintiff must, by motion, obtain consent of all parties to the action or the court's leave granted on notice to all parties to the action if it files the third-party complaint more than 90 days after service of the summons upon that defending party.
    (b) Service of Complaint with Third-Party Complaint. The third-party plaintiff must serve a copy of the plaintiff's complaint with the third-party summons and complaint.
    (c) Service on Other Parties. A copy of the third-party summons and complaint must be promptly served on all other parties to the action.

(Amended effective July 1, 2018.)

14.02. Third-Party Defendant's Claims and Defenses
    The person served with the summons and third-party complaint—the "third-party defendant":
    (A) must assert any defense against the third-party plaintiff's claim under Rule 12;
    (B) must assert any counterclaim against the third-party plaintiff under Rule 13.01 and may assert any counterclaim against the third-party plaintiff under Rule 13.02 or any crossclaim against another third-party defendant under Rule 13.07;
    (C) may assert against the plaintiff any defense that the third-party plaintiff has to the plaintiff's claim; and
    (D) may also assert against the plaintiff any claim arising out of the transaction or occurrence that is the subject matter of the plaintiff's claim against the third-party plaintiff.

(Amended effective July 1, 2018.)

14.03. Plaintiff's Claims Against a Third-Party Defendant
    The plaintiff may assert against the third-party defendant any claim arising out of the transaction or occurrence that is the subject matter of the plaintiff's claim against the third-party plaintiff. The third-party defendant must then assert any defense under Rule 12 and any counterclaim under Rule 13.01, and may assert any counterclaim under Rule 13.02 or any crossclaim under Rule 13.07. With leave of the court, the third-party defendant may assert counterclaims permitted under Rule 13.05 or Rule 13.06.

(Amended effective July 1, 2018.)

14.04. Motion to Strike, Sever, or Try Separately
    Any party may move to strike the third-party claim, to sever it, or to try it separately.

(Adopted effective July 1, 2018.)

14.05. Third-Party Defendant's Claim Against a Nonparty

A third-party defendant may proceed under this rule against a nonparty who is or may be liable to the third-party defendant for all or part of any claim against it.

(Adopted effective July 1, 2018.)

14.06. When a Plaintiff May Bring in a Third Party
When a claim is asserted against a plaintiff, the plaintiff may bring in a third party if this rule would allow a defendant to do so.

(Adopted effective July 1, 2018.)

14.07. Defending Against a Demand for Judgment for the Plaintiff
The third-party plaintiff may demand judgment in the plaintiff's favor against the third-party defendant. In that event, the third-party defendant must defend under Rule 12 against the plaintiff's claim as well as the third-party plaintiff's claim; and the action proceeds as if the plaintiff had sued both the third-party defendant and the third-party plaintiff.

(Adopted effective July 1, 2018.)

14.08. Protective Orders for Parties and Prevention of Delay

The court may make such orders to prevent a party from being embarrassed or put to undue expense, or to prevent delay of the trial or other proceeding by the assertion of a third-party claim, and may dismiss the third-party claim, order separate trials, or make other orders to prevent delay or prejudice. Unless otherwise specified in the order, a dismissal pursuant to this rule is without prejudice.

(Adopted July 1, 2018.)

Advisory Committee Comment—2018 Amendments

Rule 14 is substantially reorganized and reformatted to include paragraphing and headings. The amended rule is modeled on Fed. R. Civ. P. 14 after its restyling amendment in 2007. The committee believes that the current Rule 14.01, set forth in a single (and long) paragraph, is not particularly readable. These changes are intended to make the rule easier to use and understand, but are not intended to change the substantive interpretation of the rule. Because the rule closely follows its federal counterpart, federal court decisions on third-party practice will have greater value in interpreting the state rule.

Rule 14.08 is new in number, but identical to the former Rule 14.03, except for the change of title. "Orders for Protection" is replaced with the more familiar "Protective Orders" for limitations on discovery. This change is made to avoid confusion with restraining orders to prevent personal abuse or harassment.

RULE 15. AMENDED AND SUPPLEMENTAL PLEADINGS

15.01. Amendments

A party may amend a pleading once as a matter of course at any time before a responsive pleading is served or, if the pleading is one to which no responsive pleading is permitted and the action has not been placed upon the trial calendar, the party may so amend it at any time within 21 days after it is served. Otherwise a party may amend a pleading only by leave of court or by written consent of the adverse party; and leave shall be freely given when justice so requires. A party shall plead in response to an amended pleading within the time remaining for response to the original pleading or within 14 days after service of the amended pleading, whichever period may be longer, unless the court otherwise orders.

(Amended effective January 1, 2020.)

15.02. Amendments to Conform to the Evidence

When issues not raised by the pleadings are tried by express or implied consent of the parties, they shall be treated in all respects as if they had been raised in the pleadings. Such amendment of the pleadings as may be necessary to cause them to conform to the evidence and to raise these issues may be made upon motion of any party at any time, even after judgment; but failure so to amend does not affect the result of a trial of these issues. If evidence is objected to at the trial on the ground that it is not within the issues raised by the pleadings, the court may allow the pleadings to be amended and shall do so freely when the presentation of the merits of the action will be subserved thereby and the objecting party fails to satisfy the court that admission of such evidence would prejudice maintenance of the action or defense upon the merits. The court may grant a continuance to enable the objecting party to meet such evidence.

15.03. Relation Back of Amendments

Whenever the claim or defense asserted in the amended pleading arose out of the conduct, transaction, or occurrence set forth or attempted to be set forth in the original pleading, the amendment relates back to the date of the original pleading. An amendment changing the party against whom a claim is asserted relates back if the foregoing provision is satisfied and, within the period provided by law for commencing the action against the party, the party to be brought in by amendment (1) has received such notice of the institution of the action that the party will not be prejudiced in maintaining a defense on the merits, and (2) knew or should have known that, but for a mistake concerning the identity of the proper party, the action would have been brought against that party.

15.04. Supplemental Pleadings

Upon motion of a party the court may, upon reasonable notice and upon such terms as are just, permit the party to serve a supplemental pleading setting forth transactions, occurrences, or events which have happened since the date of the pleading sought to be supplemented, whether or not the original pleading is defective in its statement of a claim for relief or of a defense. If the court deems it advisable that the adverse party plead thereto, it shall so order, specifying the time therefor.

Advisory Committee Comment—2020 Amendments

Rule 15.01 is amended as part of the amendments made to the timing provisions of the rules. These amendments implement the adoption of a standard "day" for counting deadlines under the rules—counting all days regardless of the length of the period and standardizing the time periods, where practicable, to a 7-, 14-, 21- or 28-day schedule. The only changes to this rule lengthen the 20-day limit to 21 days, and the 10-day limit to 14 days. These change only the time limits, and are not intended to have any other effect.

RULE 16. PRETRIAL CONFERENCES; SCHEDULING; MANAGEMENT

16.01. Pretrial Conferences; Objectives

In any action, the court may in its discretion direct the attorneys for the parties and any self-represented litigants to appear before it for a conference or conferences before trial for such purposes as:
- (a) expediting the disposition of the action;
- (b) establishing early and continuing control so that the case will not be protracted because of lack of management;
- (c) discouraging wasteful pretrial activities;
- (d) improving the quality of the trial through more thorough preparation; and
- (e) facilitating the settlement of the case.

(Amended effective July 1, 2015.)

16.02. Scheduling and Planning

The court may, and upon written request of any party with notice to all parties, shall, after consulting with the attorneys for the parties and any unrepresented parties, by a scheduling conference, telephone, mail, or other suitable means, enter a scheduling order that limits the time:
- (a) to join other parties and to amend the pleadings;
- (b) to file and hear motions; and
- (c) to complete discovery.

The scheduling order also may include
- (d) provisions for disclosure or discovery of electronically stored information;

(e) any agreements the parties reach for asserting claims of privilege or of protection as trial-preparation materials after production;
(f) the date or dates for conferences before trial, a final pretrial conference, and trial; and
(g) any other matters appropriate in the circumstances of the case.

A schedule shall not be modified except by leave of court upon a showing of good cause.

(Amended effective July 1, 2007.)

16.03. Subjects for Consideration

At any conference under this rule consideration may be given, and the court may take appropriate action, with respect to:
(a) the formulation and simplification of the issues, including the elimination of frivolous claims or defenses;
(b) the necessity or desirability of amendments to the pleadings;
(c) the possibility of obtaining admissions of fact and of documents which will avoid unnecessary proof, stipulations regarding the authenticity of documents, and advance rulings from the court on the admissibility of evidence;
(d) the avoidance of unnecessary proof and of cumulative evidence, and limitations or restrictions on the use of testimony under Rule 702 of the Minnesota Rules of Evidence;
(e) the appropriateness and timing of summary adjudication under Rule 56;
(f) the control and scheduling of discovery, including orders affecting discovery pursuant to Rule 26 and Rules 29 through 37;
(g) the identification of witnesses and documents, the need and schedule for filing and exchanging pretrial briefs, and the date or dates for further conferences and for trial;
(h) the advisability of referring matters pursuant to Rule 53;
(i) settlement and the use of special procedures to assist in resolving the dispute when authorized by statute or rule;
(j) the form and substance of the pretrial order;
(k) the disposition of pending motions;
(l) the need for adopting special procedures for managing potentially difficult or protracted actions that may involve complex issues, multiple parties, difficult legal questions, or unusual proof problems;
(m) an order for a separate trial pursuant to Rule 42.02 with respect to a claim, counterclaim, cross-claim, or third-party claim, or with respect to any particular issue in the case;
(n) an order directing a party or parties to present evidence early in the trial with respect to a manageable issue that could, on the evidence, be the basis for a judgment as a matter of law under Rule 50.01 or an involuntary dismissal under Rule 41.02(b);
(o) an order establishing a reasonable limit on the time allowed for presenting evidence; and
(p) such other matters as may facilitate the just, speedy, and inexpensive disposition of the action.

At least one of the attorneys for each party participating in any conference before trial shall have authority to enter into stipulations and to make admissions regarding all matters that the participants may reasonably anticipate may be discussed. If appropriate, the court may require that a party or its representative be present or reasonably available by telephone in order to consider possible settlement of the dispute.

(Amended effective January 1, 2006.)

Advisory Committee Comments--1996 Amendments

This change conforms Rule 16.03 to its federal counterpart. The rule is expanded to enumerate many of the functions with which pretrial conferences must deal. Although the courts have inherent power to deal with these matters even in the absence of a rule, it is desirable to have the appropriate subjects for consideration at pretrial conferences expressly provided for by rule. The federal changes expressly provide for discussion of settlement, in part, to remove any confusion over the power of the court to order participation in court-related settlement efforts. See, e.g., G. Heileman Brewing Co. v. Joseph Oat Corp., 871 F.2d 648 (7th Cir. 1989); Strandell v. Jackson County, Ill. (In re Tobin), 838 F.2d 884 (7th Cir. 1988); Klothe v. Smith, 771 F.2d 667 (2d Cir. 1985); Buss v. Western Airlines, Inc., 738 F.2d 1053 (9th Cir. 1984).

Advisory Committee Comment—2006 Amendment

Rule 16.03(n) is amended to reflect the new name for motions under Rule 50.01 as amended effective January 1, 2006.

Advisory Committee Comment—2007 Amendment

Rule 16.02 is amended to allow the court to include provision for discovery of electronically stored information. Although this discovery may not require special attention in a pretrial order, in many cases it may be helpful to address this subject separately. The rule also permits the pretrial order to memorialize the court's approval of agreements relating to claims of privilege. The rule specifically contemplates that parties may desire to permit documents to be reviewed or sampled, in order to permit the requesting parties to assess the reasonable need for further production without prejudice to any privilege claims.

16.04. Final Pretrial Conference

Any final pretrial conference may be held as close to the time of trial as reasonable under the circumstances. The participants at any such conference shall formulate a plan for trial, including a program for facilitating the admission of evidence. The conference shall be attended by at least one of the attorneys who will conduct the trial for each of the parties and by any self-represented litigants.

(Amended effective July 1, 2015.)

16.05. Pretrial Orders

After any conference held pursuant to this rule, an order shall be entered reciting the action taken. This order shall control the subsequent course of the action and shall be modified only to prevent manifest injustice.

16.06. Sanctions

If a party or party's attorney fails to obey a scheduling or pretrial order, or if no appearance is made on behalf of a party at a scheduling or pretrial conference, or if a party or party's attorney is substantially unprepared to participate in the conference, or if a party or party's attorney fails to participate in good faith, the court, upon motion or upon its own initiative, may make such orders with regard thereto as are just, including any of the orders provided in Rule 37.02(b)(2), (3), (4). In lieu of or in addition to any other sanction, the court shall require the party or the attorney representing the party or both to pay the reasonable expenses incurred because of any noncompliance with this rule, including attorney fees, unless the court finds that the noncompliance was substantially justified or that other circumstances make an award of expenses unjust.

IV. PARTIES

RULE 17. PARTIES PLAINTIFF AND DEFENDANT; CAPACITY

17.01. Real Party in Interest

Every action shall be prosecuted in the name of the real party in interest. An executor, administrator, guardian, bailee, trustee of an express trust, a party with whom or in whose name a contract has been made for the benefit of another, or a party authorized by statute may sue in that person's own name without joining the party for whose benefit the action is brought. No action shall be dismissed on the ground that it is not prosecuted in the name of the real party in interest until a reasonable time has been allowed after objection for ratification of commencement of the action by, or joinder or substitution of, the real party in interest; and such ratification, joinder, or substitution shall have the same effect as if the action had been commenced in the name of the real party in interest.

17.02. Infants or Incompetent Persons

Whenever a party to an action is an infant or is incompetent and has a representative duly appointed under the laws of this state or the laws of a foreign state or country, the representative may sue or defend on behalf of such party. A party who is an infant or is incompetent and is not so represented shall be represented by a guardian ad litem appointed by the court in which the action is pending or is to be brought. The guardian ad litem shall be a resident of this state, shall file a consent and oath with the court administrator, and shall give such bond as the court may require. A guardian ad litem appointed under this Rule is not a guardian ad litem within the meaning of the Rules of Guardian Ad Litem Procedure in Juvenile and Family Court and is not governed by those Rules.

Any person, including an infant party over the age of 14 years and under no other legal disability, may apply under oath for the appointment of a guardian ad litem. The application of the party or the party's spouse or parents or testamentary or other guardian shall have priority over other applications. If no such appointment is made on behalf of a defendant party before answer or default, the adverse party or a party's attorney may apply for such appointment, and in such case the court shall allow the guardian ad litem a reasonable time to respond to the complaint.

The application for appointment shall show (1) the name, age and address of the party, (2) if the party is a minor, the names and addresses of the parents, and, in the event of their death or the abandonment of the minor, the name and address of the party's custodian or testamentary or other guardian, if any, (3) the name and address of the party's spouse, if any, and (4) the name, age, address, and occupation of the person whose appointment is sought.

If the appointment is applied for by the party or by a spouse, parent, custodian or testamentary or other guardian of the party, the court may hear the application with or without notice. In all other cases written notice of the hearing on the application shall be given at such time as the court shall prescribe, and shall be served upon the party, the party's spouse, parent, custodian and testamentary or other guardian, if any, and if the party is an inmate of a public institution, the chief executive officer thereof. If the party is a nonresident or, after diligent search, cannot be found within the state, notice shall be given to such persons and in such manner as the court may direct.

RULE 18. JOINDER OF CLAIMS AND REMEDIES

18.01. Joinder of Claims

A party asserting a claim to relief as an original claim, counterclaim, cross-claim, or third-party claim, may join, either as independent or as alternate claims, as many claims, legal, or equitable, as the party has against an opposing party.

18.02. Joinder of Remedies; Fraudulent Conveyances

Whenever a claim is one heretofore cognizable only after another claim has been prosecuted to a conclusion, the two claims may be joined in a single action; but the court shall grant relief in that action only in accordance with the relative substantive rights of the parties. In particular, a plaintiff may state a claim for money and a claim to have set aside a conveyance fraudulent as to that plaintiff, without first having obtained a judgment establishing the claim for money.

RULE 19. JOINDER OF PERSONS NEEDED FOR JUST ADJUDICATION

19.01. Persons to be Joined if Feasible

A person who is subject to service of process shall be joined as a party in the action if (a) in the person's absence complete relief cannot be accorded among those already parties, or (b) the person claims an interest relating to the subject of the action and is so situated that the disposition of the action in the person's absence may (1) as a practical matter impair or impede the person's ability to protect that interest or (2) leave any one already a party subject to a substantial risk or incurring double, multiple, or otherwise inconsistent obligations by reason of the person's claimed interest. If the person has not been so joined, the court shall order that the person be made a party. If the person should join as a plaintiff but refuses to do so, the person may be made a defendant, or, in a proper case, an involuntary plaintiff.

19.02. Determination by Court Whenever Joinder Not Feasible

If a person as described in Rule 19.01 cannot be made a party, the court shall determine whether in equity and good conscience the action should proceed among the parties before it, or should be dismissed, the absent person being thus regarded as indispensable. The factors to be considered by the court include:
- (a) to what extent a judgment rendered in the person's absence might be prejudicial to the person or those already parties;
- (b) the extent to which, by protective provisions in the judgment, by the shaping of relief, or other measures, the prejudice can be lessened or avoided;
- (c) whether a judgment rendered in the person's absence will be adequate; and
- (d) whether the plaintiff will have an adequate remedy if the action is dismissed for nonjoinder.

19.03. Pleading Reasons for Nonjoinder

A pleading asserting a claim for relief shall state the names, if known to the pleader, of any persons as described in Rule 19.01 who are not joined, and the reasons why they are not joined.

19.04. Exception of Class Actions

This rule is subject to the provisions of Rule 23.

RULE 20. PERMISSIVE JOINDER OF PARTIES

20.01. Permissive Joinder

All persons may join in one action as plaintiffs if they assert any right to relief, jointly, severally, or in the alternative with respect to or arising out of the same transaction, occurrence, or series of transactions or occurrences and if any question of fact or law common to all these persons will arise in the action. All persons may be joined in one action as defendants if there is asserted against them jointly, severally, or in the alternative, any right to relief with respect to or arising out of the same transaction, occurrence, or series of transactions or occurrences and if any question of law or fact common to all defendants will arise in the action. A plaintiff or defendant need not be interested in obtaining or defending against all the relief demanded. Judgment may be given for one or more of the plaintiffs according to their respective rights to relief, and against one or more defendants according to their respective liabilities.

20.02. Separate Trials

The court may make such order as will prevent a party from being embarrassed, delayed, or put to expense by the inclusion of a party against whom the party asserts no claim and who asserts no claim against the party, and may order separate trials or make other orders to prevent delay or prejudice.

RULE 21. MISJOINDER AND NONJOINDER OF PARTIES

Misjoinder of parties is not ground for dismissal of an action. Parties may be dropped or added by order of the court on motion of any party or upon the court's own initiative at any stage of the action and on such terms as are just. Any claim against a party may be severed and proceeded with separately.

RULE 22. INTERPLEADER

Persons having claims against the plaintiff may be joined as defendants and required to interplead, in an action brought for that purpose, when their claims are such that the plaintiff is or may be exposed to multiple liability. A defendant exposed to similar liability may obtain such interpleader by way of cross-claim or counterclaim. If such a defendant admits being subject to liability, that defendant may, upon paying the amount claimed or delivering the property claimed or its value into court or to such person as the court may direct, move for an order to substitute the claimants other than the plaintiff as defendants in the movant's stead. On compliance with the terms of such order, the defendant shall be discharged and the action shall proceed against the substituted defendants. It is not ground for objection to such joinder or to such motion that the claims of the several claimants or the titles on which their claims depend do not have a common origin or are not identical with but are adverse to and independent of one another, or that the plaintiff denies liability in whole or in part to any or all of the claimants. The provisions of this rule do not restrict the joinder of parties permitted in Rule 20.

RULE 23. CLASS ACTIONS

23.01. Prerequisites to a Class Action

One or more members of a class may sue or be sued as representative parties on behalf of all only if
      (a)   the class is so numerous that joinder of all members is impracticable;
      (b)   there are questions of law or fact common to the class;

(c) the claims or defenses of the representative parties are typical of the claims or defenses of the class; and

(d) the representative parties will fairly and adequately protect the interests of the class.

23.02. Class Actions Maintainable

An action may be maintained as a class action if the prerequisites of Rule 23.01 are satisfied, and in addition:

(a) the prosecution of separate actions by or against individual members of the class would create a risk of
   (1) inconsistent or varying adjudications with respect to individual members of the class which would establish incompatible standards of conduct for the party opposing the class, or
   (2) adjudications with respect to individual members of the class which would as a practical matter be dispositive of the interests of the other members not parties to the adjudications or substantially impair or impede their ability to protect their interests; or

(b) the party opposing the class has acted or refused to act on grounds generally applicable to the class, thereby making appropriate final injunctive relief or corresponding declaratory relief with respect to the class as a whole; or

(c) the court finds that the questions of law or fact common to the members of the class predominate over any questions affecting only individual members, and that a class action is superior to other available methods for the fair and efficient adjudication of the controversy. The matters pertinent to the findings include:
   (1) the interest of members of the class in individually controlling the prosecution or defense of separate actions;
   (2) the extent and nature of any litigation concerning the controversy already commenced by or against members of the class;
   (3) the desirability or undesirability of concentrating the litigation of the claims in the particular forum; and
   (4) the difficulties likely to be encountered in the management of a class action.

23.03. Determining by Order Whether to Certify a Class Action; Appointing Class Counsel; Notice and Membership in Class; Judgment; Multiple Classes and Subclasses

(a) **Certification Order.**

   (1) When a person sues or is sued as a representative of a class, the court must—at an early practicable time—determine by order whether to certify the action as a class action.
   (2) An order certifying a class action must define the class and the class claims, issues, or defenses, and must appoint class counsel under Rule 23.07.
   (3) An order under Rule 23.03(a)(1) may be altered or amended before final judgment.

(b) **Notice.**

(1) For any class certified under Rule 23.02(a) or (b), the court may direct appropriate notice to the class.

(2) For any class certified under Rule 23.02(c), the court must direct to class members the best notice practicable under the circumstances, including individual notice to all members who can be identified through reasonable effort. The notice must concisely and clearly state in plain, easily understood language:
  (A) the nature of the action,
  (B) the definition of the class certified,
  (C) the class claims, issues, or defenses,
  (D) that a class member may enter an appearance through counsel if the member so desires,
  (E) that the court will exclude from the class any member who requests exclusion, stating when and how members may elect to be excluded, and
  (F) the binding effect of a class judgment on class members under Rule 23.03(c).

(c) **Identification of Class Members.** The judgment in an action maintained as a class action under Rule 23.02(a) or (b), whether or not favorable to the class, shall include and describe those whom the court finds to be members of the class. The judgment in an action maintained as a class action under Rule 23.02(c), whether or not favorable to the class, shall include and specify or describe those to whom the notice provided in Rule 23.03(b) was directed, and who have not requested exclusion, and whom the court finds to be members of the class.

(d) **Issue Classes and Subclasses.** When appropriate (1) an action may be brought or maintained as a class action with respect to particular issues, or (2) a class may be divided into subclasses and each subclass treated as a class; the provisions of this rule shall then be construed and applied accordingly.

23.04. Orders in Conduct of Action

In the conduct of actions to which this rules applies, the court may make appropriate orders:
(a) determining the course of proceedings or prescribing measures to prevent undue repetition or complication in the presentation of evidence or argument;
(b) requiring, for the protection of the members of the class or otherwise for the fair conduct of the action, that notice be given in such manner as the court may direct to some or all members of any step in the action, or of the proposed extent of the judgment, or of the opportunity of members to signify whether they consider the representation fair and adequate, to intervene and present claims or defenses, or otherwise to enter the action;
(c) imposing conditions on the representative parties or intervenors;
(d) requiring that the pleadings be amended to eliminate therefrom allegations as to representation of absent persons, and that the action proceed accordingly; or

(e) dealing with similar procedural matters.

The orders may be combined with an order pursuant to Rule 16, and may be altered or amended whenever necessary.

23.05. Settlement, Voluntary Dismissal, or Compromise

(a) **Court Approval.**

(1) A settlement, voluntary dismissal, or compromise of the claims, issues, or defenses of a certified class is effective only if approved by the court.
(2) The court must direct notice in a reasonable manner to all class members who would be bound by a proposed settlement, voluntary dismissal, or compromise.
(3) The court may approve a settlement, voluntary dismissal, or compromise that would bind class members only after a hearing and on finding that the settlement, voluntary dismissal, or compromise is fair, reasonable, and adequate.

(b) **Disclosure Required.** The parties seeking approval of a settlement, voluntary dismissal, or compromise under Rule 23.05(a) must file a statement identifying any agreement made in connection with the proposed settlement, voluntary dismissal, or compromise.

(c) **Additional Opt-Out Period.** In an action previously certified as a class action under Rule 23.02(c), the court may refuse to approve a settlement unless it affords a new opportunity to request exclusion to individual class members who had an earlier opportunity to request exclusion but did not do so.

(d) **Objection to Settlement.**

(1) Any class member may object to a proposed settlement, voluntary dismissal, or compromise that requires court approval under Rule 23.05(a)(1).
(2) An objection made under Rule 23.05(d)(1) may be withdrawn only with the court's approval.

(e) **Distribution of Residual Funds, If Any.**

In the event there are residual funds that remain after payment of all approved class member claims (including any supplemental distributions to the class), expenses, litigation costs, attorney's fees, and other court-approved disbursements, the court shall direct notice regarding the distribution of these funds. This notice shall be provided to any potential recipient of residual funds identified by the parties or the court and to the Legal Services Advisory Committee for the purpose of informing qualified legal services programs within the meaning of Minnesota Statutes § 480.24, subdivision 3.

In approving the distribution or other disposition of residual funds, the district court shall consider all relevant factors, including the recommendations of the parties, the nexus between the nature, purpose, and objectives of the class action and the interests of the class members, and the interests of potential recipients of the residual funds.

(Amended effective July 1, 2018.)

Rule 23.06. Appeals

The court of appeals may in its discretion permit an appeal from an order of a district court granting or denying class action certification under this rule. An application to appeal must be sought within the time provided in Rule 105 of the Minnesota Rules of Civil Appellate Procedure, and shall be subject to the other provisions of that rule. An appeal does not stay proceedings in the district court unless the district judge or the court of appeals so orders.

Rule 23.07. Class Counsel

(a) **Appointing Class Counsel.**

(1) Unless a statute provides otherwise, a court that certifies a class must appoint class counsel.
(2) An attorney appointed to serve as class counsel must fairly and adequately represent the interests of the class.
(3) In appointing class counsel, the court
  (A) must consider:
    (i) the work counsel has done in identifying or investigating potential claims in the action,
    (ii) counsel's experience in handling class actions, other complex litigation, and claims of the type asserted in the action,
    (iii) counsel's knowledge of the applicable law, and
    (iv) the resources counsel will commit to representing the class;
  (B) may consider any other matter pertinent to counsel's ability to fairly and adequately represent the interests of the class;
  (C) may direct potential class counsel to provide information on any subject pertinent to the appointment and to propose terms for attorney fees and nontaxable costs; and
  (D) may make further orders in connection with the appointment.

(b) **Appointment Procedure.**

    (1) The court may designate interim counsel to act on behalf of the putative class before determining whether to certify the action as a class action.

    (2) When there is one applicant for appointment as class counsel, the court may appoint that applicant only if the applicant is adequate under Rule 23.07(a)(2) and (3). If more than one adequate applicant seeks appointment as class counsel, the court must appoint the applicant best able to represent the interests of the class.

    (3) The order appointing class counsel may include provisions about the award of attorney fees or nontaxable costs under Rule 23.08.

Rule 23.08. Attorney Fees Award

In an action certified as a class action, the court may award reasonable attorney fees and nontaxable costs authorized by law or by agreement of the parties as follows:

(a) **Motion for Award of Attorney Fees.** A claim for an award of attorney fees and nontaxable costs must be made by motion, subject to the provisions of this subdivision, at a time set by the court. Notice of the motion must be served on all parties and, for motions by class counsel, directed to class members in a reasonable manner.

(b) **Right to Object.** A class member, or a party from whom payment is sought, may object to the motion.

(c) **Hearing and Findings.** The court may hold a hearing and must find the facts and state its conclusions of law on the motion under Rule 52.01.

(d) **Reference to Special Master.** The court may refer issues related to the amount of the award to a special master as provided in Rule 53.01(a).

23.09. Derivative Actions by Shareholders or Members

In a derivative action brought by one or more shareholders or members to enforce a right of a corporation or of an unincorporated association, the corporation or association having failed to enforce a right which may properly be asserted by it, the complaint shall allege that the plaintiff was a shareholder or member at the time of the transaction of which the plaintiff complains or that the plaintiff's share or membership thereafter devolved on the plaintiff by operation of law. The complaint shall also allege with particularity the efforts, if any, made by the plaintiff to obtain the desired action from the directors or comparable authority and, if necessary, from the shareholders or members, and the reasons for the plaintiff's failure to obtain the action or for not making the effort. The derivative action may not be maintained if it appears that the plaintiff does not fairly and adequately represent the interest of the shareholders or members similarly situated in enforcing the right of the corporation or association. The action shall not be dismissed or compromised without the approval of the court, and notice of the proposed dismissal or compromise shall be given to shareholders or members in such manner as the court directs.

23.10. Actions Relating to Unincorporated Associations

An action brought by or against the members of an unincorporated association as a class by naming certain members as representative parties may be maintained only if it appears that the representative parties will fairly and adequately protect the interests of the association and its members. In the conduct of the action the court may make appropriate orders corresponding with those described in Rule 23.04 and the procedure for dismissal or compromise of the action shall correspond with that provided in Rule 23.05.

Advisory Committee Comment—2006 Amendments

Rule 23 is extensively revamped by these amendments. The recommended changes primarily adopt the amendments made to federal rule 23 in 2003. The reasons for these amendments are set forth in the advisory committee notes that accompanied the federal rule amendments. See Fed. R. Civ. P. 23, Advis. Comm. Notes—2003 Amends., reprinted in Fed. Civ. Jud. Proc. & Rules 132-37 (West 2005 ed.). Those notes provide useful information on the purposes for these amendments and may be consulted for interpretation of these rules.

Rule 23.03(a)(1) requires class certification to be taken up "at an early practicable time" rather than "as soon as practicable." Although these standards are substantially similar, the former rule's phrasing occasionally prompted courts to feel they did not have the leeway to defer ruling on certification until a later, more logical time. In many cases, certification cannot be decided without consideration of the practicalities of trying the case, making early certification impractical. See generally Manual for Complex Litigation (Fourth) § 21.133 (Fed. Jud. Ctr. 2004). Rule 23.03(a)(2) places in the rule an express requirement that the class be defined at the time of certification and that class counsel be appointed. Precise definition of the class is necessary to identify the persons entitled to relief, bound by a judgment in the case, and entitled to notice. Id. § 21.222. The procedures for appointment of class counsel are set forth in Rule 23.07. The rule omits reference to a "conditional" certification, reflecting the disfavor this device has earned, but preserves the ability of courts to amend a certification order any time before final judgment is entered.

Rule 23.03(b) establishes the power of the court to direct notice to the class in actions certified under Rule 23.02(a) or (b) (where notice is not generally required) and also states the requirement that notice be given to members of classes certified under Rule 23.02(c). Rule 23.03(b)(2) provides guidance on the content and form of these required notices, and requires the use of plain language. Sample plain-language class notice documents are available on the Federal Judicial Center's website, http://www.fjc.gov. These requirements are intended to improve the amount of useful information available to potential class members and to inform their decision on class participation.

Rule 23.05 is expanded to define the procedures for review and approval of class settlements. The rule adopts the changes in Fed. R. Civ. P. 23(e) with one stylistic modification. The federal rule, read literally, might appear to suggest that a trial court must approve every settlement submitted for approval; the language is reworked in the proposed rule to make it clear that although court approval is required for a settlement to be effective, the court's options are not constrained. Indeed, many proposed settlements are properly rejected for not being in the interest of class members. Rule 23.05(a)(3) requires that a hearing be held, and Rule 23.05(b) creates an express requirement that any "side" agreements relating to the settlement must be identified in a statement filed with the court. Rule 23.05(a)(1) removes an ambiguity that existed under the old rule, and now expressly requires court approval only of claims of a certified class.

Rule 23.05(c) authorizes the court to allow a "second opt-out" right in actions certified under Rule 23.02(c). In these actions an opt-out deadline is typically established early in the period following certification. This provision allows the court to permit class members who have not opted out to do so with knowledge of the actual settlement terms.

Rule 23.06 makes it clear that decisions relating to class certification are subject to appellate review on a discretionary basis. This rule is slightly different from its federal counterpart because Minnesota has an established process for discretionary appeals of interlocutory orders, Minn. R. Civ. App. P. 105, that is not present in the federal system. This new provision does not substantially change existing Minnesota practice, as the Minnesota appellate courts have allowed discretionary appeals under Rule 105. See, e.g., Gordon v. Microsoft Corp., 645 N.W.2d 393 (Minn. 2002). The federal rule adopts a shorter 10-day deadline for seeking appellate review of decisions relating to class certification decisions. The committee believes that consistency with the requirements for other discretionary appeals in Minnesota is more important than consistency with the federal rule on this point. The other provisions of Rule 105 and the appellate rules generally apply to appeals under Rule 23.06.

RULE 24. INTERVENTION

24.01. Intervention of Right

Upon timely application anyone shall be permitted to intervene in an action when the applicant claims an interest relating to the property or transaction which is the subject of the action and the applicant is so situated that the disposition of the action may as a practical matter impair or impede the applicant's ability to protect that interest, unless the applicant's interest is adequately represented by existing parties.

24.02. Permissive Intervention

Upon timely application anyone may be permitted to intervene in an action when an applicant's claim or defense and the main action have a common question of law or fact. When a party to an action relies for ground of claim or defense upon any statute or executive order administered by a federal or state governmental officer or agency or upon any regulation, order, requirement, or agreement issued or made pursuant to the statute or executive order, the officer or agency upon timely application may be permitted to intervene in the action. In exercising its discretion, the court shall consider whether the intervention will unduly delay or prejudice the adjudication of the rights of the original parties.

24.03. Procedure

A person desiring to intervene shall serve on all parties to the action and file a notice of intervention which shall state that in the absence of objection by an existing party to the action within 30 days after service thereof upon the party, such intervention shall be deemed to have been accomplished. The notice of intervention shall be accompanied by a pleading setting forth the nature and extent of every claim or defense as to which intervention is sought and the reasons for the claim of entitlement to intervention. Within 30 days after service upon the party seeking to intervene of a notice of objection to intervention, the party shall serve a motion to intervene upon all parties as provided in Rule 5.

Upon written consent of all parties to the action, anyone interested may intervene under this rule without notice.

[24.04. Notice to Attorney General -- deleted effective July 1, 2007.]

Advisory Committee Comment--1993 Amendments

The only change made to this rule is to correct a typographical or grammatical error in the existing rule. No change in meaning or interpretation is intended.

Advisory Committee Comment—2007 Amendment

Rule 24.04 is deleted because the subject matter is now addressed by new Rule 5A.

RULE 25. SUBSTITUTION OF PARTIES

25.01. Death

(a) If a party dies and the claim is not extinguished or barred, the court may order substitution of the proper parties. The motion for substitution may be made by the successors or representatives of the deceased party or by any party and, together with the notice of hearing, shall be served on the parties as provided in Rule 5 and upon persons not parties in the manner provided in Rule 4 for the service of process.

(b) In the event of the death of one or more of the plaintiffs or of one or more of the defendants in an action in which the right sought to be enforced survives only to the surviving plaintiffs or only against the surviving defendants, the action does not abate. The death shall be indicated upon the record and the action shall proceed in favor of or against the surviving parties.

25.02. Incompetency

If a party becomes incompetent, the action shall not abate because of the disability, and the court upon motion served as provided in Rule 25.01 may allow it to be continued by or against the party's representative.

25.03. Transfer of Interest

In case of any transfer of interest, the action may be continued by or against the original party, unless the court upon motion directs the person to whom the interest is transferred to be substituted in the action or joined with the original party. Service of this motion shall be made as provided in Rule 25.01.

25.04. Public Officers; Death or Separation from Office

When any public officer is a party to an action and during its pendency dies, resigns, or otherwise ceases to hold office, the action may be continued and maintained by or against the officer's successor if it is satisfactorily shown to the court that there is a substantial need for so continuing and maintaining it. Substitution pursuant to this rule may be made when it is shown by supplemental pleading that the successor of any officer adopts or continues or threatens to adopt or continue the action of the officer's predecessor. Before a substitution is made, the party or officer to be affected, unless expressly assenting thereto, shall be given reasonable notice of the application therefor and accorded an opportunity to object.

V. DEPOSITIONS AND DISCOVERY

RULE 26. DUTY TO DISCLOSE; GENERAL PROVISIONS GOVERNING DISCOVERY

26.01. Required Disclosures

(a) **Initial Disclosure**.

    (1) In General. Except as exempted by Rule 26.01(a)(2) or as otherwise stipulated or ordered by the court, a party must, without awaiting a discovery request, provide to the other parties:

        (A) the name and, if known, the address and telephone number of each individual likely to have discoverable information—along with the subjects of that information—that the disclosing party may use to support its claims or defenses, unless the use would be solely for impeachment;

        (B) a copy—or a description by category and location—of all documents, electronically stored information, and tangible things that the disclosing party has in its possession, custody, or control and may use to support its claims or defenses, unless the use would be solely for impeachment;

        (C) a computation of each category of damages claimed by the disclosing party—who must also make available for inspection and copying as under Rule 34 the documents or other evidentiary material, unless privileged or protected from disclosure, on which each computation is based, including materials bearing on the nature and extent of injuries suffered; and

        (D) for inspection and copying as under Rule 34, any insurance agreement under which an insurance business may be liable to satisfy all or part of a possible judgment in the action or to indemnify or reimburse for payments made to satisfy the judgment.

(2) Proceedings Exempt from Disclosure. Unless otherwise ordered by the court in an action, the following proceedings are exempt from disclosures under Rule 26.01(a), (b), and (c):
(A) an action for review on an administrative record;
(B) a forfeiture action in rem arising from a state statute;
(C) a petition for habeas corpus or any other proceeding to challenge a criminal conviction or sentence;
(D) an action brought without an attorney by a person in the custody of the United States, a state, or a state subdivision;
(E) an action to enforce or quash an administrative summons or subpoena;
(F) a proceeding ancillary to a proceeding in another court;
(G) an action to enforce an arbitration award;
(H) family court actions under Gen. R. Prac. 301 - 378;
(I) Torrens actions;
(J) conciliation court appeals;
(K) forfeitures;
(L) removals from housing court to district court;
(M) harassment proceedings;
(N) name change proceedings;
(O) default judgments;
(P) actions to either docket a foreign judgment or re-docket a judgment within the district;
(Q) appointment of trustee;
(R) condemnation appeal;
(S) confession of judgment;
(T) implied consent;
(U) restitution judgment; and
(V) tax court filings.

(3) Time for Initial Disclosures—In General. A party must make the initial disclosures at or within 60 days after the original due date when an answer is required, unless a different time is set by stipulation or court order, or unless an objection is made in a proposed discovery plan submitted as part of a civil cover sheet required under Rule 104 of the General Rules of Practice for the District Courts. In ruling on the objection, the court must determine what disclosures, if any, are to be made and must set the time for disclosure.

(4) Time for Initial Disclosures—For Parties Served or Joined Later. A party that is first served or otherwise joined after the initial disclosures are due under Rule 26.01(a)(3) must make the initial disclosures within 30 days

after being served or joined, unless a different time is set by stipulation or court order.

(5) Basis for Initial Disclosure; Unacceptable Excuses. A party must make its initial disclosures based on the information then reasonably available to it. A party is not excused from making its disclosures because it has not fully investigated the case or because it challenges the sufficiency of another party's disclosures or because another party has not made its disclosures.

(b) **Disclosure of Expert Testimony**.

(1) In General. In addition to the disclosures required by Rule 26.01(a), a party must disclose to the other parties the identity of any witness it may use at trial to present evidence under Minnesota Rule of Evidence 702, 703, or 705.

(2) Witnesses Who Must Provide a Written Report. Unless otherwise stipulated or ordered by the court, this disclosure must be accompanied by a written report—prepared and signed by the witness—if the witness is one retained or specially employed to provide expert testimony in the case or one whose duties as the party's employee regularly involve giving expert testimony. The report must contain:
  (A) a complete statement of all opinions the witness will express and the basis and reasons for them;
  (B) the facts or data considered by the witness in forming them;
  (C) any exhibits that will be used to summarize or support them;
  (D) the witness's qualifications, including a list of all publications authored in the previous 10 years;
  (E) a list of all other cases in which, during the previous 4 years, the witness testified as an expert at trial or by deposition; and
  (F) a statement of the compensation to be paid for the study and testimony in the case.

(3) Witnesses Who Do Not Provide a Written Report. Unless otherwise stipulated or ordered by the court, if the witness is not required to provide a written report, this disclosure must state:
  (A) the subject matter on which the witness is expected to present evidence under Minnesota Rule of Evidence 702, 703, or 705; and
  (B) a summary of the facts and opinions to which the witness is expected to testify.

(4) Time to Disclose Expert Testimony. A party must make these disclosures at the times and in the sequence that the court orders. Absent a stipulation or a court order, the disclosures must be made:
  (A) at least 90 days before the date set for trial or for the case to be ready for trial; or
  (B) if the evidence is intended solely to contradict or rebut evidence on the same subject matter identified by another party under Rule 26.01(b)(2) or (3), within 30 days after the other party's disclosure.

(5) Supplementing the Disclosure. The parties must supplement these disclosures when required under Rule 26.05.

(c) **Pretrial Disclosures**.

(1) In General. In addition to the disclosures required by Rule 26.01(a) and (b), a party must provide to the other parties the following information about the evidence that it may present at trial other than solely for impeachment:
  (A) the name and, if not previously provided, the address and telephone number of each witness—separately identifying those the party expects to present and those it may call if the need arises;
  (B) the designation of those witnesses whose testimony the party expects to present by deposition and, if not taken stenographically, a transcript of the pertinent parts of the deposition; and
  (C) an identification of each document or other exhibit, including summaries of other evidence—separately identifying those items the party expects to offer and those it may offer if the need arises.

(2) Time for Pretrial Disclosures; Objections. Unless the court orders otherwise, these disclosures must be made at least 30 days before trial. Within 14 days after they are made, unless the court sets a different time, a party may serve and promptly file a list of the following objections: any objections to the use under Rule 32.01 of a deposition designated by another party under Rule 26.01(c)(1)(B); and any objection, together with the grounds for it, that may be made to the admissibility of materials identified under Rule 26.01(c)(1)(C). An objection not so made—except for one under Minnesota Rule of Evidence 402 or 403—is waived unless excused by the court for good cause.

(d) **Form of Disclosures**. Unless the court orders otherwise, all disclosures under Rule 26.01 must be in writing, signed, and served.

(Amended effective July 1, 2013.)

26.02. Discovery Methods, Scope and Limits

Unless otherwise limited by order of the court in accordance with these rules, the methods and scope of discovery are as follows:

(a) **Methods.** Parties may obtain discovery by one or more of the following methods: depositions by oral examination or written questions; written interrogatories; production of documents or things or permission to enter upon land or other property; for inspection and other purposes; physical (including blood) and mental examinations; and requests for admission.

(b) **Scope and Limits.** Unless otherwise limited by court order, the scope of discovery is as follows. Parties may obtain discovery regarding any nonprivileged matter that is relevant to any party's claim or defense and proportional to the needs of the case, considering the importance of the issues at stake in the action, the amount in controversy, the parties' relative access to relevant information, the parties' resources, the importance of the discovery in resolving the issues, and whether the burden or expense of the proposed discovery outweighs its likely benefit. Information within this scope of discovery need not be admissible in evidence to be discoverable.

(1) <u>Authority to Limit Frequency and Extent</u>. The court may establish or alter the limits on the number of depositions and interrogatories and may also limit the length of depositions under Rule 30 and the number of requests under Rule 36. The court may act upon its own initiative after reasonable notice or pursuant to a motion under Rule 26.03.

(2) <u>Limits on Electronically Stored Evidence for Undue Burden or Cost</u>. A party need not provide discovery of electronically stored information from sources that the party identifies as not reasonably accessible because of undue burden or cost. On motion to compel discovery or for a protective order, the party from whom discovery is sought must show that the information is not reasonably accessible because of undue burden or cost. If that showing is made, the court may nonetheless order discovery from such sources if the requesting party shows good cause and proportionality, considering the limitations of Rule 26.02(b)(3). The court may specify conditions for the discovery.

(3) <u>Limits Required When Cumulative; Duplicative; More Convenient Alternative; and Ample Prior Opportunity</u>. The frequency or extent of use of the discovery methods otherwise permitted under these rules shall be limited by the court if it determines that:
  (i) the discovery sought is unreasonably cumulative or duplicative, or is obtainable from some other source that is more convenient, less burdensome, or less expensive; or
  (ii) the party seeking discovery has had ample opportunity by discovery in the action to obtain the information sought; or
  (iii) the burden of proposed discovery is outside the scope permitted by Rule 26.02(b).

The court may act upon its own initiative after reasonable notice or pursuant to a motion under Rule 26.03.

(c) **Insurance Agreements.** In any action in which there is an insurance policy that may afford coverage, any party may require any other party to disclose the coverage and limits of such insurance and the amounts paid and payable thereunder and, pursuant to Rule 34, may obtain production of the insurance policy; provided, however, that this provision will not permit such disclosed information to be introduced into evidence unless admissible on other grounds.

(d) **Trial Preparation: Materials.** Subject to the provisions of Rule 26.02(e) a party may obtain discovery of documents and tangible things otherwise discoverable pursuant to Rule 26.02(b) and prepared in anticipation of litigation or for trial by or for another party or by or for that other party's representative (including the other party's attorney, consultant, surety, indemnitor, insurer, or agent) only upon a showing that the party seeking discovery has substantial need of the materials in the preparation of the party's case and that the party is unable without undue hardship to obtain the substantial equivalent of the materials by other means. In ordering discovery of such materials when the required showing has been made, the court shall protect against disclosure of the mental impressions, conclusions, opinions, or legal theories of an attorney or other representative of a party concerning the litigation.

A party may obtain without the required showing a statement concerning the action or its subject matter previously made by that party. Upon request, a party or other person may obtain without the required showing a statement concerning the action or its subject matter previously made by that person who is not a party. If the request is refused, the person may move for a court order. The provisions of Rule 37.01(d) apply to the award of expenses incurred in relation to the motion. For purposes of this paragraph, a statement previously made is (1) a written statement signed or otherwise adopted or approved by the person making it, or (2) a stenographic, mechanical, electrical, or other recording, or a transcription thereof, that is a substantially verbatim recital of an oral statement by the person making it and contemporaneously recorded.

(e) **Trial Preparation: Experts.** Discovery of facts known and opinions held by experts, otherwise discoverable pursuant to Rule 26.02(b) and acquired or developed in anticipation of litigation or for trial, may be obtained only as follows:

(1) (A) A party may through interrogatories require any other party to identify each person whom the other party expects to call as an expert witness at trial, to state the subject matter on which the expert is expected to testify, and to state the substance of the facts and opinions to which the expert is expected to testify and a summary of the grounds for each opinion. (B) Upon motion, the court may order further discovery by other means, subject to such restrictions as to scope and such provisions, pursuant to Rule 26.02(e)(3), concerning fees and expenses, as the court may deem appropriate.

(2) A party may discover facts known or opinions held by an expert who has been retained or specially employed by another party in anticipation of litigation or preparation for trial and who is not expected to be called as a witness at trial, only as provided in Rule 35.02 or upon a showing of exceptional circumstances under which it is impracticable for the party seeking discovery to obtain facts or opinions on the same subject by other means.

(3) Unless manifest injustice would result, (A) the court shall require the party seeking discovery to pay the expert a reasonable fee for time spent in responding to discovery pursuant to Rules 26.02(e)(1)(B) and 26.02(e)(2);

and (B) with respect to discovery obtained pursuant to Rule 26.02(e)(1)(B), the court may require, and with respect to discovery obtained pursuant to Rule 26.02(e)(2) the court shall require, the party seeking discovery to pay the other party a fair portion of the fees and expenses reasonably incurred by the latter party in obtaining facts and opinions from the expert.

(f) **Claims of Privilege or Protection of Trial Preparation Materials.**

(1) When a party withholds information otherwise discoverable under these rules by claiming that it is privileged or subject to protection as trial preparation material, the party shall make the claim expressly and shall describe the nature of the documents, communications, or things not produced or disclosed in a manner that, without revealing information itself privileged or protected, will enable other parties to assess the applicability of the privilege or protection.

(2) If information is produced in discovery that is subject to a claim of privilege or of protection as trial-preparation material, the party making the claim may notify any party that received the information of the claim and the basis for it. After being notified, a party must promptly return, sequester, or destroy the specified information and any copies it has and may not use or disclose the information until the claim is resolved. A receiving party may promptly present the information to the court under seal for a determination of the claim. If the receiving party disclosed the information before being notified, it must take reasonable steps to retrieve it. The producing party must preserve the information until the claim is resolved.

(Amended effective July 1, 2018.)

Advisory Committee Comment—2006 Amendment

The amendment to Rule 26.02 is simple but potentially quite important. The rule is amended to conform to Fed. R. Civ. P. 26(b) as amended in 2000. Although the proposed changes were expected to create as many problems as they solved, see, e.g., John S. Beckerman, Confronting Civil Discovery's Fatal Flaws, 84 Minn. L. Rev. 505, 537-43 (2000); Jeffrey W. Stempel & David F. Herr, Applying Amended Rule 26(b)(1) in Litigation: The New Scope of Discovery, in 199 F.R.D. 396 (2001), the change in the scope of discovery, to limit it to the actual claims and defenses raised in the pleadings, has worked well in federal court, and most feared problems have not materialized. See generally Thomas D. Rowe, Jr., A Square Peg in a Round Hole? The 2000 Limitation on the Scope of Federal Civil Discovery, 69 Tenn. L. Rev. 13, 25-27 (2001); Note, The Sound and the Fury or the Sound of Silence?: Evaluating the Pre-Amendment Predictions and Post-Amendment Effects of the Discovery Scope-Narrowing Language in the 2000 Amendments to Federal Rule of Civil Procedure 26(b)(1), 37 Ga. L. Rev. 1039 (2003). Courts have simply not found the change dramatic nor given it a draconian interpretation. See, e.g., Sanyo Laser Prod., Inc. v. Arista Records, Inc., 214 F.R.D. 496 (S.D. Ind. 2003).

The narrowing of the scope of discovery as a matter of right does not vitiate in any way the traditional rule that discovery should be liberally allowed. It should be limited to the claims and defenses raised by the pleadings, but the requests should still be liberally construed. See, e.g., Graham v. Casey's General Stores, 206 F.R.D. 251, 253 (S.D. Ind. 2002) ("Even after the recent amendments to Federal Rule of Civil Procedure 26, courts employ a liberal discovery standard.").

Advisory Committee Comment—2007 Amendment

Rule 26.02(b)(2) is a new provision that establishes a two-tier standard for discovery of electronically stored information. The rule makes information that is not "reasonably accessible because of undue burden or cost" not normally discoverable. This rule is identical to its federal counterpart, adopted in 2006. The rule requires that it be identified in response to an appropriate request, but if it is identified as "not reasonably accessible," it need not be produced in the absence of further order. It is not strictly exempt from discovery, as the court may, upon motion that "shows good cause," order disclosure of the information. The rule explicitly authorizes the court to impose conditions on any order for disclosure of this information, and conditions that either ease the undue burden or minimize the total cost or cost borne by the producing party would be appropriate.

Rule 26.02(f)(2) is a new provision that creates a uniform procedure for dealing with assertions of privilege that are made following production of information in discovery. The rule creates a mandatory obligation to return, sequester, or destroy information that is produced in discovery if the producing party asserts that it is subject to a privilege or work-product protection. The information cannot be used for any purpose until the privilege claim is resolved. The rule provides a mechanism for the receiving party to have the validity of the privilege claim resolved by the court. The rule does not create any presumption or have any impact on the validity of the claim of privilege, nor does it excuse the inadvertent or regretted production. If the court determines that that production waived an otherwise valid privilege, then the information should be ordered for production or release from sequestration of the information.

Advisory Committee Comment—2018 Amendments

Rule 26.02 is amended to adopt the changes made to Fed. R. Civ. P. 26(b) in 2015. The amendments are intended to improve the operation of the rule and to avoid some of the problems that were encountered under the former rule.

26.03. Protective Orders

(a) In General. Upon motion by a party or by the person from whom discovery is sought, and for good cause shown, the court in which the action is pending or alternatively, on matters relating to a deposition, the court in the district where the deposition is to be taken may make any order which justice requires to protect a party or person from annoyance, embarrassment, oppression, or undue burden or expense, including one or more of the following:

(1) that the discovery not be had;
(2) that the discovery may be had only on specified terms and conditions, including a designation of the time or location or the allocation of expenses, for the disclosure or discovery;
(3) that the discovery may be had only by a method of discovery other than that selected by the party seeking discovery;

(4) that certain matters not be inquired into, or that the scope of the discovery be limited to certain matters;

(5) that discovery be conducted with no one present except persons designated by the court;

(6) that a deposition, after being sealed, be opened only by order of the court;

(7) that a trade secret or other confidential research, development, or commercial information not be disclosed or be disclosed only in a designated way; or

(8) that the parties simultaneously file specified documents or information enclosed in sealed envelopes to be opened as directed by the court.

(b) Ordering Discovery. If the motion for a protective order is denied in whole or in part, the court may, on such terms and conditions as are just, order that any party or person provide or permit discovery. Rule 37.01(d) applies to the award of expenses incurred in connection with the motion.

(c) Awarding Expenses. Rule 37.01(d) applies to the award of expenses incurred in connection with the motion.

(Amended effective July 1, 2018.)

Advisory Committee Comment—2018 Amendments

Rule 26.03 is amended to adopt a change made to Fed. R. Civ. P. 26(c) in 2015. The amendment explicitly provides that cost-shifting is one option available to the court in implementing protective relief, where appropriate. The rule is not intended to make cost-shifting a routine part of discovery motions, but recognizes that there are some situations where it is appropriate. The rule is also subdivided and numbered to make it easier to use and cite; the headings are not intended to affect the interpretation of the rule.

26.04. Timing and Sequence of Discovery

(a) **Timing**. Notwithstanding the provisions of Rules 26.02, 30.01, 31.01(a), 33.01(a), 36.01, and 45, parties may not seek discovery from any source before the parties have conferred and prepared a discovery plan as required by Rule 26.06(c) except in a proceeding exempt from initial disclosure under Rule 26.01(a)(2), or when allowed by stipulation or court order.

(b) Early Rule 34 Requests.

(1) Time to Deliver. More than 21 days after the summons and complaint are served on a party, a request under Rule 34 may be delivered:
(A) to that party by any other party, and
(B) by that party to any plaintiff or to any other party that has been served.

(2) When Considered Served. The request is considered to have been served when the parties have conferred and prepared a discovery plan as required by Rule 26.06(c).

(c) **Sequence**. Unless the court upon motion, for the convenience of parties and witnesses and in the interests of justice, orders otherwise, methods of discovery may be used in any sequence and the fact that a party is conducting discovery, whether by deposition or otherwise, shall not operate to delay any other party's discovery.

(d) **Expedited Litigation Track**. Expedited timing and modified content of certain disclosure and discovery obligations may be required by order of the supreme court adopting special rules for the pilot expedited civil litigation track.

(Amended effective July 1, 2018.)

Advisory Committee Comment—2018 Amendments

Rule 26.04 is amended to adopt a change made to Fed. R. Civ. P. 26(d) in 2015, which allows the service of Rule 34 requests before other discovery is permitted. The rule permits a party responding to the request additional time to prepare an appropriate response, but does not compel earlier response or production. The service of an earlier request may also provide earlier notice to a party of the need to preserve evidence for use in the case, and thus eliminate some disputes over spoliation of evidence. The effect of the rule is to authorize earlier service of Rule 34 requests but the rule does not allow a serving party to accelerate the response deadline by doing so.

26.05. Supplementation of Responses

A party who has responded to a request for discovery is under a duty to supplement or correct the response to include information thereafter acquired if ordered by the court or in the following circumstances:

A party is under a duty seasonably to amend a prior response to an interrogatory, request for production, or request for admission if the party learns that the response is in some material respect incomplete or incorrect and if the additional or corrective information has not otherwise been made known to the other parties during the discovery process or in writing. With respect to testimony of an expert, the duty extends to information contained in interrogatory responses, in any report of the expert, and to information provided through a deposition of the expert.

(Amended effective July 1, 2000.)

26.06. Discovery Conference and Discovery Plan.

(a) **Conference Timing.** Except in a proceeding exempted from initial disclosure under Rule 26.01(a)(2) or when the court orders otherwise, the parties must confer as soon as practicable—and in any event within 30 days from the initial due date for an answer.

(b) **Conference Content; Parties' Responsibilities**. In conferring, the parties must consider the nature and basis of their claims and defenses and the possibilities for promptly settling or resolving the case; make or arrange for the disclosures required by Rule 26.01(a), (b); discuss any issues about preserving discoverable information; and develop a proposed discovery plan. The attorneys of record and all self-represented litigants that have appeared in the case are jointly responsible for arranging the conference, and for attempting in good faith to agree on the proposed discovery plan. A written report outlining the discovery plan must be filed with the court within 14 days after the conference or at the time the action is filed, whichever is later. The court may order the parties or attorneys to attend the conference in person.

(c) **Discovery Plan**. A discovery plan must state the parties' views and proposals on:
    (1) what changes should be made in the timing, form, or requirement for disclosures under Rule 26.01, including a statement of when initial disclosures were made or will be made;
    (2) the subjects on which discovery may be needed, when discovery should be completed, and whether discovery should be conducted in phases or be limited to or focused on particular issues;
    (3) any issues about disclosure, discovery, or preservation of electronically stored information, including the form or forms in which it should be produced;
    (4) any issues about claims of privilege or of protection as trial-preparation materials, including—if the parties agree on a procedure to assert these claims after production—whether to ask the court to include their agreement in an order;
    (5) what changes should be made in the limitations on discovery imposed under these rules or by local rule, and what other limitations should be imposed; and
    (6) any other orders that the court should issue under Rule 26.03 or under Rule 16.02 and .03.

(d) **Conference with the Court**. At any time after service of the summons, the court may direct the attorneys for the parties to appear before it for a conference on the subject of discovery. The court shall do so upon motion by the attorney for any party if the motion includes:
    (1) A statement of the issues as they then appear;
    (2) A proposed plan and schedule of discovery;
    (3) Any issues relating to disclosure or discovery of electronically stored information, including the form or forms in which it should be produced;
    (4) Any issues relating to claims of privilege or of protection as trial-preparation material, including—if the parties agree on a procedure to assert such claims after production—whether to ask the court to include their agreement in an order.
    (5) Any limitations proposed to be placed on discovery;
    (6) Any other proposed orders with respect to discovery; and
    (7) A statement showing that the attorney making the motion has made a reasonable effort to reach agreement with opposing attorneys on the matter

set forth in the motion. All parties and attorneys are under a duty to participate in good faith in the framing of any proposed discovery plan.

Notice of the motion shall be served on all parties. Objections or additions to matters set forth in the motion shall be served not later than 14 days after the service of the motion.

Following the discovery conference, the court shall enter an order tentatively identifying the issues for discovery purposes, establishing a plan and schedule for discovery, setting limitations on discovery, if any, and determining such other matters, including the allocation of expenses, as are necessary for the proper management of discovery in the action. An order may be altered or amended whenever justice so requires.

Subject to the right of a party who properly moves for a discovery conference to prompt convening of the conference, the court may combine the discovery conference with a pretrial conference authorized by Rule 16.

(Amended effective January 1, 2020.)

Advisory Committee Comment—2007 Amendment

Rule 26.06 is amended to add to the required provisions in a motion for a discovery conference. These changes require the party seeking a discovery conference to address electronic discovery issues, but do not dictate any particular resolution or conference agenda for them. Many cases will not involve electronic discovery issues, and there is no need to give substantial attention to them in a request for a conference under this rule.

Advisory Committee Comment—2018 Amendments

Rule 26.06(c) is amended to provide expressly for inclusion of preservation of evidence as a subject to be addressed in the discovery plan in every case. This requirement recognizes both the importance of document-preservation issues and the benefits of addressing the issue early in the case.

Advisory Committee Comment—2020 Amendments

Rule 26.06(d) is amended as part of the extensive amendments made to the timing provisions of the rules. These amendments implement the adoption of a standard "day" for counting deadlines under the rules—counting all days regardless of the length of the period and standardizing the time periods, where practicable, to a 7-, 14-, 21- or 28-day schedule. The only change to this rule lengthens the 10-day limit to 14 days to respond to a motion for a discovery conference. This change affects only the time limit, and is not intended to have any other effect.

26.07. Signing of Discovery Requests, Responses and Objections

In addition to the requirements of Rule 33.01(d), every request for discovery or response or objection thereto made by a party represented by an attorney shall be signed by at least one attorney of record in the attorney's individual name, whose address and e-mail address shall be stated. A self-represented litigant shall sign the request, response, or objection and state the party's address and e-mail address. The signature constitutes a certification that the attorney or party has read the request, response, or objection, and that to the best of the signer's knowledge, information and belief formed after a reasonable inquiry it is:

(1) consistent with these rules and warranted by existing law or a good faith argument for the extension, modification, or reversal of existing law;

(2) not interposed for any improper purpose, such as to harass or to cause unnecessary delay or needless increase in the cost of litigation; and

(3) not unreasonable or unduly burdensome or expensive, given the needs of the case, the discovery had in the case, the amount in controversy, and the importance of the issues at stake in the litigation.

If a request, response, or objection is not signed, it shall be stricken unless it is signed promptly after the omission is called to the attention of the party making the request, response or objection and a party shall not be obligated to take any action with respect to it until it is signed.

If a certification is made in violation of this rule, the court, upon motion or upon its own initiative, shall impose upon the person who made the certification, the party on whose behalf the request, response, or objection is made, or both, an appropriate sanction, which may include an order to pay the amount of the reasonable expenses incurred because of the violation, including reasonable attorney fees.

(Amended effective July 1, 2015.)

Advisory Committee Comments--2000 Amendments

The changes made to Rule 26 include some of the recent amendments to the federal rule made in 1993. The changes made to the Minnesota rule have been modified to reflect the fact that Minnesota practice does not include the automatic disclosure mechanisms that have been adopted in some federal courts; the resulting differences in the rules are minor, and the authorities construing the federal rule should be given full weight to the extent applicable.

The changes in Rule 26.02(a) adopt similar amendments made to FED. R. CIV. P. 26(b) in 1993. The new rule is intended to facilitate greater judicial control over the extent of discovery. The rule does not limit or curtail any form of discovery or establish numeric limits on its use, but does clarify the broad discretion courts have to limit discovery.

Rule 26.02(e) is a new rule adopted directly from its federal counterpart. The requirement of a privilege log is necessary to permit consideration, by opposing counsel and ultimately by the courts, of the validity of privilege claims. Privilege logs have been in use for years and are routinely required when a dispute arises. See generally Nevada Power Co. v. Monsanto Co., 151 F.R.D. 118, 122 & n.6 (D. Nev. 1993) (enumerating deficiencies in log); Allendale Mutual Ins. Co. v. Bull Data Sys., Inc., 145 F.R.D. 84 (N.D. Ill. 1992) (ordering privilege log and specifying requirements); Grossman v. Schwarz, 125 F.R.D. 376, 386-87 (S.D.N.Y. 1989) (holding failure to provide privilege log deemed "presumptive evidence" claim of privilege not meritorious). The requirement of the log should not, however, be an invitation to require detailed identification of every privileged document within an obviously privileged category. Courts should not require a log in all circumstances, especially where a request seeks broad categories of non-discoverable information. See, e.g., Durkin v. Shields (In re Imperial Corp. of Am.), 174 F.R.D. 475 (S.D. Cal. 1997)(recognizing document-by-document log would be unduly burdensome). It is the intention of the rule, however, to require the production of logs routinely to encourage the earlier resolution of privilege disputes and to discourage baseless assertions of privilege.

FED. R. CIV. P. 45(d)(2) expressly requires production of a privilege log by a non-party seeking to assert a privilege in response to a subpoena. Although the Committee does not recommend adoption of the extensive changes that have been made in federal Rule 45, this recommendation is made to minimize disruption in existing Minnesota subpoena practice. The difference in rules should not prevent a court from ordering production of a privilege log by a non-party in appropriate cases. The cost of producing a privilege log may be properly shifted to the party serving the subpoena under Rule 45.06.

Rule 26.05 is amended to adopt in Minnesota the same supplementation requirement as exists in federal court. It is a more stringent and more explicit standard, and reflects a sounder analysis of when supplementation is necessary. It states affirmatively the duty to disclose. The Committee believes it is particularly desirable to have state supplementation practice conform to federal practice in order that compliance with the requirements is more common and sanctions can more readily be imposed for failure to supplement. The rule relaxes the supplementation requirement to obviate supplementation where the information has been disclosed either in discovery (i.e., in other discovery responses or by deposition testimony) or in writing. The writing need not be a discovery response, and could be a letter to all counsel identifying a witness or correcting a prior response.

RULE 27. DEPOSITION BEFORE ACTION OR PENDING APPEAL

27.01. Before Action

(a) **Petition.** A person who desires to perpetuate testimony regarding any matter may file a verified petition in the district court of the county of the residence of an expected adverse party. The petition shall be entitled in the name of the petitioner and shall show

(1) that the petitioner expects to be a party to an action but is presently unable to bring it or cause it to be brought;

(2) the subject matter of the expected action and the petitioner's interest therein;

(3) the facts which the petitioner desires to establish by the proposed testimony and the reasons for desiring to perpetuate it;

(4) the names or a description of the persons the petitioner expects will be adverse parties and their addresses so far as known; and

(5) the names and addresses of the persons to be examined and the substance of the testimony which the petitioner expects to elicit from each.

The petition shall ask for an order authorizing the petitioner to take the deposition of those persons to be examined as named in the petition, for the purpose of perpetuating their testimony.

(b) **Notice and Service.** The petitioner shall thereafter serve a notice upon each person named in the petition as an expected adverse party, together with a copy of the petition, stating that the petitioner will apply to the court, at a time and place named therein, for the order described in the petition. At least 21 days before the date of hearing, the notice shall be served either within or outside the state in the manner provided in Rule 4.03 for service of summons; but if such service cannot with due diligence be made upon any expected adverse party named in the petition, the court may make such order as is just for service by publication or otherwise, and shall appoint, for persons not served in the manner provided in Rule 4.03, an attorney who shall represent them, and, in case they are not otherwise represented, shall cross-examine the deponent. If any expected adverse party is a minor or incompetent, the provisions of Rule 17.02 apply.

(c) **Order and Examination.** If the court is satisfied that the perpetuation of testimony may prevent a failure or delay of justice, it shall make an order designating and describing the persons whose depositions may be taken and specifying the subject matter of the examination and whether the depositions shall be taken upon oral examination or written interrogatories. The deposition may then be taken in accordance with these rules and the court may make orders authorized by Rules 34 and 35. For the purpose of applying these rules to depositions for perpetuating testimony, each reference therein to the court in which the action is pending shall be deemed to refer to the court in which the petition for such deposition was filed.

(d) **Use of Deposition.** If a deposition to perpetuate testimony is taken pursuant to these rules or if, although not so taken, it would be admissible in evidence in the courts of the state in which it is taken, it may be used in any action involving the same subject matter subsequently brought in this state, in accordance with the provisions of Rule 32.01.

(Amended effective January 1, 2020.)

27.02. Pending Appeal

If an appeal has been taken from a judgment or order, or before the taking of an appeal if the time therefor has not expired, the district court in which the judgment or order was rendered may allow the taking of the deposition of witnesses to perpetuate their testimony for use in the event of further proceedings in the district court. In such case, the party who desires to perpetuate the testimony may make a motion in the district court for leave to take the depositions, upon the same notice and service thereof as if the action was pending in the district court. The motion shall show the names, addresses, the substance of the testimony expected to be elicited from each person to be examined, and the reasons for perpetuating their testimony. If the court finds that the perpetuation of the testimony is proper to avoid a failure or delay of justice, it may make an order allowing the depositions to be taken and may make orders authorized by Rules 34 and 35, and thereupon the depositions may be taken and used in the same manner and under the same conditions as are prescribed in these rules for depositions taken in actions pending in the district court.

27.03. Perpetuation by Action

This rule does not limit the power of the court to entertain an action to perpetuate testimony.

Advisory Committee Comment—2020 Amendments

Rule 27.01(b) is amended as part of the extensive amendments made to the timing provisions of the rules. These amendments implement the adoption of a standard "day" for counting deadlines under the rules—counting all days regardless of the length of the period and standardizing the time periods, where practicable, to a 7-, 14-, 21- or 28-day schedule. The only change to this rule lengthens the 20-day notice requirement before hearing a petition to 21 days. This change affects only the time limits, and is not intended to have any other effect.

RULE 28. PERSONS BEFORE WHOM DEPOSITIONS MAY BE TAKEN

28.01. Within the United States

Within the United States or within a territory or insular possession subject to the jurisdiction of the United States, depositions shall be taken before an officer authorized to administer oaths by the laws of the United States or of the place where the examination is held, or before a person appointed by the court in which the action is pending. The term "officer" as used in Rules 28, 30, 31, and 32 includes a person appointed by the court or designated by the parties pursuant to Rule 29. A person so appointed has power to administer oaths and take testimony.

28.02. In Foreign Countries

Depositions may be taken in a foreign country (1) pursuant to any applicable treaty or convention, or (2) pursuant to a letter of request (whether or not captioned a letter rogatory), or (3) on notice before a person authorized to administer oaths in the place where the examination is held, either by the law thereof or by the law of the United States, or (4) before a person commissioned by the court, and a person so commissioned shall have the power by virtue of the commission to administer any necessary oath and take testimony. A commission or a letter of request shall be issued on application and notice and on terms that are just and appropriate. It is not requisite to the issuance of a commission or a letter of request that the taking of the deposition in any other manner is impracticable or inconvenient; and both a commission and a letter of request may be issued in proper cases. A notice or commission may designate the person before whom the deposition is to be taken either by name or descriptive title. A letter of request may be addressed "To the Appropriate Authority in [here name the country]." When a letter of request or any other device is used pursuant to any applicable treaty or convention, it shall be captioned in the form prescribed by that treaty or convention. Evidence obtained in response to a letter of request need not be excluded merely because it is not a verbatim transcript, because the testimony was not taken under oath, or because of any similar departure from the requirements for depositions taken within the United States under these rules.

(Amended effective January 1, 1997.)

Advisory Committee Comments--1996 Amendments

This change conforms the rule to its federal counterpart. The committee believes it is especially desirable to have this rule identical to the federal rule because of its subject matter. In addition to the usual factors favoring uniformity, this is a provision governed largely by federal law and which may need to be understood and applied by court reporters, consular or embassy officials, and other non-lawyers. Conformity to the federal rule increases the prospects that the rule will be followed and will not impose significant additional burdens on the litigants.

28.03. Disqualification for Interest

No deposition shall be taken before or reported by any person who is a relative or employee or attorney or counsel of any of the parties, or is a relative or employee of such attorney or counsel, or is financially interested in the action, or who has a contract with the party, attorney, or person with an interest in the action that affects or has a substantial tendency to affect impartiality.

RULE 29. STIPULATIONS REGARDING DISCOVERY PROCEDURE

Unless otherwise directed by the court the parties may by stipulation (1) provide that depositions may be taken before any person, at any time or place, upon any notice, and in any manner, and when so taken may be used like other depositions, and (2) modify other procedures governing or limitations placed upon discovery, except that stipulations extending the time provided in Rules 33, 34, and 36 for responses to discovery may, if they would interfere with any time set for completion of discovery, for hearing of a motion, or for trial, be made only with the approval of the court.

(Amended effective January 1, 1997.)

Advisory Committee Comments--1996 Amendments

This change conforms the rule to its federal counterpart. The committee believes it is desirable to permit stipulations regarding discovery whenever those stipulations do not impact the court's handling of the action. Particularly in state court practice, it is often necessary to extend discovery deadlines--without affecting other case management deadlines--and the parties should be encouraged to do so. Counsel agreeing to discovery after a deadline should not expect court assistance in enforcing discovery obligations nor should non-completion affect any other motions, hearings, or other case management procedures.

RULE 30. DEPOSITIONS UPON ORAL EXAMINATION

30.01. When Depositions May Be Taken

After service of the summons, any party may take the testimony of any person, including a party, by deposition upon oral examination. Leave of court, granted with or without notice, must be obtained only if the plaintiff seeks to take a deposition prior to the expiration of 30 days after service of the summons and complaint upon any defendant or service made pursuant to Rule 4.04, except that leave is not required if a defendant has served a notice of taking deposition or otherwise sought discovery. The attendance of witnesses may be compelled by subpoena as provided in Rule 45.

(Amended effective July 1, 2007.)

Advisory Committee Comment—2007 Amendment

Rule 30.01 is amended only to delete a reference to a notice procedure in former Rule 30.02(b), which was abrogated in 1996. The amendment merely conforms the rule to the current procedure.

30.02. Notice of Examination: General Requirements: Special Notice; Non-Stenographic Method of Recording; Production of Documents and Things; Deposition of Organization; Depositions by Telephone

(a) **Notice.** A party desiring to take the deposition of any person upon oral examination shall give reasonable notice in writing to every other party to the action. The notice shall state the name and place for taking the deposition and the name and address of each person to be examined, if known, and, if the name is not known, a general description sufficient to identify the person or the particular class or group to which the person belongs. If a subpoena duces tecum is to be served on the person to be examined, the designation of the materials to be produced as set forth in the subpoena shall be attached to or included in the notice.

(b) **Notice of Method of Recording.** The party taking the deposition shall state in the notice the method by which the testimony shall be recorded. Unless the court orders otherwise, it may be recorded by sound, sound-and-visual, or stenographic means, the party taking the deposition shall bear the cost of the recording. Any party may arrange for a transcription to be made from the recording of a deposition taken by non-stenographic means.

(c) **Additional Recording Method.** With prior notice to the deponent and other parties, any party may designate another method to record the deponent's testimony in addition to the method specified by the person taking the deposition. The additional record or transcript shall be made at that party's expense unless the court otherwise orders.

Any deposition pursuant to these rules may be taken by means of simultaneous audio and visual electronic recording without leave of court or stipulation of the parties if the deposition is taken in accordance with the provisions of this rule. In addition to the specific provisions of this rule, the taking of video depositions is governed by all other rules governing the taking of depositions unless the nature of the video deposition makes compliance impossible or unnecessary.

(d) **Role of Officer.** Unless otherwise agreed by the parties, a deposition shall be conducted before an officer appointed or designated under Rule 28 and shall begin with a statement on the record by the officer that includes (A) the officer's name and business address; (B) the date, time, and place of the deposition; (C) the name of the deponent; (D) the administration of the oath or affirmation to the deponent; and (E) an identification of all persons present. If the deposition is recorded other than stenographically, the officer shall repeat items (A) through (C) at the beginning of each unit of recorded tape or other recording medium. The appearance or demeanor of deponents or attorneys shall not be distorted through camera or sound-recording techniques. At the end of the deposition, the officer shall state on the record that the deposition is complete and shall set forth any stipulations made by counsel concerning the custody of the transcript or recording and the exhibits, or concerning other pertinent matters.

(e) **Production of Documents.** The notice to a party deponent may be accompanied by a request made in compliance with Rule 34 for the production of documents and tangible things at the taking of the deposition. The procedure of Rule 34 shall apply to the request.

(f) **Deposition of Organization.** A party may in the party's notice and in a subpoena name as the deponent a public or private corporation or a partnership, association, or governmental agency and describe with reasonable particularity the matters on which examination is requested. In that event, the organization so named shall designate one or more officers, directors, or managing agents, or other persons who consent to testify on its behalf, and may set forth, for each person designated, the matters on which the person will testify. A subpoena shall advise a non-party organization of its duty to make such a designation. The persons so designated shall testify as to matters known or reasonably available to the organization. This provision does not preclude taking a deposition by any other procedure authorized in these rules.

(g) **Telephonic Depositions.** The parties may stipulate in writing or the court may upon motion order that a deposition be taken by telephone or other remote electronic means. For the purposes of this rule and Rules 28.01, 37.01(a), 37.02(a) and 45.03, a deposition taken by such means is taken in the district and at the place where the deponent is to answer questions.

(Amended effective January 1, 2006.)

Advisory Committee Comment--1993 Amendments

Rule 30.02(d)(1) is amended to change slightly the arrangements for handling the videotape record of a deposition taken by that means. At the present time the rule requires the videotape operator to retain possession of the videotape, a circumstance which sometimes makes it difficult to procure the videotape for use at a trial which takes place long after the deposition was taken. The amendment directs the lawyer for the party taking the deposition to retain custody of the video recording after it has been sealed and marked for identification purposes. This procedure is consistent with the procedure for handling original typewritten deposition transcripts pursuant to Minn. R. Civ. P. 30.06(a).

When the Advisory Committee recommended the addition of Rule 30.02(h) in 1988, the members of the committee hoped that it would be a useful device for curbing discovery abuses, but it appears that the rule is almost never used. The deletion of this portion of the rule should not be taken as any support for expanded discovery. The authority to control discovery is amply set forth in other rules, see, e.g., Minn. Gen. R. Prac. 111 & 112, and the committee encourages the continued vigorous exercise of this authority for the protection of all litigants and to carry out the mandate of Minn. R. Civ. P. 1, which provides that the Rules of Civil Procedure "shall be construed to secure the just, speedy, and inexpensive determination of every action."

Advisory Committee Comment—2006 Amendment

Rule 30.02 is amended only to add subsection titles. This change is made for convenience and consistency with the style of other rules, and is not intended to affect the rule's interpretation. Rule 30.02(g) is amended to renumber one of the rule cross-references to reflect the amendment and renumbering of Rule 45 as part of the amendments effective January 1, 2006.

30.03. Examination and Cross-Examination; Record of Examination; Oath; Objections

Examination and cross-examination of witnesses may proceed as permitted at the trial under the provisions of the Minnesota Rules of Evidence except Rules 103 and 615. The officer before whom the deposition is to be taken shall put the witness on oath or affirmation and shall personally, or by someone acting under the officer's direction and in the officer's presence, record the testimony of the witness. The testimony shall be taken stenographically or recorded by any other means ordered in accordance with Rule 30.02(d). If requested by one of the parties, the testimony shall be transcribed.

All objections made at the time of the examination to the qualifications of the officer taking the deposition, to the manner of taking it, to the evidence presented, to the conduct of any party, or to any other aspect of the proceedings shall be noted by the officer upon the deposition; but the examination shall proceed, with the testimony being taken subject to the objections. In lieu of participating in the oral examination, a party may serve written questions in a sealed envelope on the party taking the deposition and the party taking the deposition shall transmit them to the officer, who shall propound them to the witness and record the answers verbatim.

(Amended effective January 1, 1997.)

30.04. Schedule and Duration; Motion to Terminate or Limit Examination

(a) **Objections.** Any objection to evidence during a deposition shall be stated concisely and in a non-argumentative and non-suggestive manner. A person may instruct a deponent not to answer only when necessary to preserve a privilege, to enforce a limitation on evidence directed by the court, or to present a motion under paragraph (d).

(b) **Duration.** Unless otherwise authorized by the court or stipulated by the parties, a deposition is limited to one day of seven hours. The court must allow additional time consistent with Rule 26.02(a) if needed for a fair examination of the deponent or if the deponent or another person, or other circumstance, impedes or delays the examination.

(c) **Sanctions.** If the court finds such an impediment, delay, or other conduct that has frustrated the fair examination of the deponent, it may impose upon the persons responsible an appropriate sanction, including the reasonable costs and attorney's fees incurred by any parties as a result thereof.

(d) **Suspension of Examination.** At any time during a deposition, on motion of a party or of the deponent and upon a showing that the examination is being conducted in bad faith or in such manner as unreasonably to annoy, embarrass, or oppress the deponent or party, the court in which the action is pending or the court in the district where the deposition is being taken may order the officer conducting the examination to cease forthwith from taking the deposition, or may limit the scope and manner of the taking of the deposition as provided in Rule 26.03. If the order made terminates the examination, it shall be resumed thereafter only upon the order of the court in which the action is pending. Upon demand of the objecting party or deponent, the taking of the deposition shall be suspended for the time necessary to make a motion for an order. The provisions of Rule 37.01(d) apply to the award of expenses incurred in relation to the motion.

(Amended effective January 1, 2006.)

Advisory Committee Comment—2006 Amendment

Rule 30.04(a) is amended to remove an ambiguity in the current rule. As amended, the rule expressly extends the prohibition against improper instruction of a deponent not to answer to all persons (including counsel for a non-party witness), instead of just "parties."

Rule 30.04(b) is amended to adopt a specific time limit on depositions. Although parties may agree to a longer deposition and the court can determine that longer examination is appropriate, a deposition is made subject to a limit of one day lasting seven hours. This amendment is identical to the change in Fed. R. Civ. P. 30(d)(2) made in 2000. The purpose of this amendment is to decrease the burden of discovery on witnesses and to encourage focused examination of all deponents. Where the examining party engages in proper and focused examination and encounters unhelpful responses or inappropriate objections, or where the issues in the case dictate that additional time is necessary to permit a fair examination, the court is required to provide it. The rule establishes a presumptive limit on the length of depositions, not the presumptive length. Most depositions will continue to be much shorter than seven hours, and the rule does not limit courts from establishing shorter time limits in particular cases.

30.05. Review by Witness; Changes; Signing

If requested by the deponent or a party before completion of the deposition, the deponent shall have 30 days after being notified by the officer that the transcript or recording is available in which to review the transcript or recording and, if there are changes in form or substance, to sign a statement reciting such changes and the reasons given by the deponent for making them. The officer shall indicate in the certificate prescribed by Rule 30.06(a) whether any review was requested and, if so, shall append any changes made by the deponent during the period allowed.

(Amended effective July 1, 2018.)

30.06. Certification and Filing by Officer; Exhibits; Copies; Notices of Filing

    (a)   **Certification by Officer; Exhibits.** The officer shall certify that the witness was duly sworn by the officer and that the deposition is a true record of the testimony given by the witness, and shall certify that the deposition has been transcribed, that the cost of the original has been charged to the party who noticed the deposition, and that all parties who ordered copies have been charged at the same rate for such copies. This certificate shall be in writing and accompany the record of the deposition. Unless otherwise ordered by the court or agreed to by the parties the officer shall securely seal the deposition in an envelope or package endorsed with the title of the action and marked "Deposition of (herein insert the name of witness)," and shall promptly send it to the attorney or party who arranged for the transcript or recording, who shall store it under conditions that will protect it against loss, destruction, tampering, or deterioration. Documents and things produced for inspection during the examination of the witness shall, upon the request of a party, be marked for identification and annexed to the deposition and may be inspected and copied by any party, except that if the person producing the materials desires to retain them, the person may (1) offer copies to be marked for identification and annexed to the deposition and to serve thereafter as originals if the person affords to all parties fair opportunity to verify the copies by comparison with the originals, or (2) offer the originals to be marked for identification after giving each party an opportunity to inspect and copy them, in which event the materials may then be used in the same manner as if annexed to the deposition. Any party may move for an order that the original be annexed to and returned with the deposition pending final disposition of the case.

    (b)   **Duties of Officer.** Unless otherwise ordered by the court or agreed by the parties, the officer shall retain stenographic notes of any deposition taken stenographically or a copy of the recording of any deposition taken by another method. Upon payment of reasonable charges therefor, the officer shall furnish a copy of the transcript or other recording of the deposition to any party or to the deponent.

(c) **Notice of Receipt of Transcript.** The party taking the deposition shall give prompt notice of its receipt from the officer to all other parties.

(Amended effective January 1, 2006.)

Advisory Committee Comments--1996 Amendments

These amendments substantially conform the rule to its federal counterpart. The committee believes it is particularly desirable to have the rules governing the mechanics of taking depositions conform to the federal rules because many depositions are taken for use in parallel state and federal proceedings or in distant locations before reporters who can be expected to know the federal procedures but may not know idiosyncratic Minnesota rules.

Rule 30.04 is largely new and includes important provisions governing the conduct of depositions. Most important is Rule 30.04(a), which is intended to constrain the conduct of attorneys at depositions. The rule limits deposition objections to concise statements that are directed to the record and not so suggesting a possible answer to the deponent. This rule is intended to set a high standard for conduct of depositions. The problem of deposition misconduct, though probably not as severe as has been noted in some reported cases, is still a frequent and unfortunate part of Minnesota practice. See, e.g., Hall v. Clifton Precision, 150 F.R.D. 525 (E.D. Pa. 1993); Paramount Communications, Inc. v. QVC Network, Inc., 637 A.2d 34, 51-57 (Del. 1994); Kelvey v. Coughlin, 625 A.2d 775 (R.I. 1993).

Rule 30.06 is amended to follow its federal counterpart, retaining the existing mechanism for delivering transcripts of depositions to the lawyer or party noticing the deposition rather than filing them with the court. This difference is necessary because Minn. R. Civ. P. 5.04 does not permit filing discovery in the absence of an order.

Advisory Committee Comment—2006 Amendment

Rule 30.06 is amended only to add subsection titles. This change is made for convenience and consistency with the style of other rules, and is not intended to affect the rule's interpretation

30.07. Failure to Attend or to Serve Subpoena; Expenses

(a) **Failure of Party Noticing Deposition to Attend.** If the party giving the notice of the taking of a deposition fails to attend and proceed therewith and another party attends in person or by attorney pursuant to the notice, the court may order the party giving the notice to pay to such other party the amount of the reasonable expenses incurred by the other party and the other party's attorney in so attending, including reasonable attorney fees.

(b) **Failure to Serve Subpoena on Non-Party Witness.** If the party giving the notice of the taking of a deposition of a witness fails to serve a subpoena upon that witness, and the witness because of such failure does not attend, and if another party attends in person or by attorney on the expectation that the deposition of that witness is to be taken, the court may order the party giving notice to pay to such other party the amount of the reasonable expenses incurred by those individuals in so attending, including reasonable attorney fees.

Advisory Committee Comment—2006 Amendment

Rule 30.07 is amended only to add subsection titles. This change is made for convenience and consistency with the style of other rules, and is not intended to affect the rule's interpretation

RULE 31. DEPOSITIONS OF WITNESSES UPON WRITTEN QUESTIONS

31.01 Serving Questions; Notice

(a) A party may take the testimony of any person, including a party, by deposition upon written questions without leave of court except as provided in paragraph (b). The attendance of witnesses may be compelled by the use of subpoena as provided in Rule 45.

(b) A party must obtain leave of court, which shall be granted to the extent consistent with the principles stated in Rule 26.02(b), if the person to be examined is confined in prison or if, without the written stipulation of the parties, the person to be examined has already been deposed in the case.

(c) A party desiring to take a deposition upon written questions shall serve them upon every other party with a notice stating (1) the name and address of the person who is to answer them, if known, and if the name is not known, a general description sufficient to identify the person or the particular class or group to which the person belongs, and (2) the name or descriptive title and address of the officer before whom the deposition is to be taken. A deposition upon written questions may be taken of a public or private corporation or a partnership or association or governmental agency in accordance with the provisions of Rule 30.02(f).

(d) Within 14 days after the notice and written questions are served, a party may serve cross questions upon all other parties. Within 7 days after being served with cross questions, a party may serve redirect questions upon all other parties. Within 7 days after being served with redirect questions, a party may serve recross questions upon all other parties. The court may for cause shown enlarge or shorten the time.

(Amended effective July 1, 2018.)

Advisory Committee Comment—2018 Amendments

Rule 31.01(a) is amended to correct the cross-reference to paragraph 2(b) of the rule. Rule 31.01(b) is similarly amended only to correct the cross-reference to the correct paragraph of Rule 26.02. These amendments are not intended to change the operation or interpretation of either rule.

31.02 Officer to Take Responses and Prepare Record

A copy of the notice and copies of all questions served shall be delivered by the party taking the deposition to the officer designated in the notice, who shall proceed promptly, in the manner provided by Rules 30.03, 30.05, and 30.06, to take the testimony of the witness in response to the questions and to prepare, certify, and file or mail the deposition, attaching thereto the copy of the notice and the questions received by the officer.

(Amended effective January 1, 1997.)

Advisory Committee Comments--1996 Amendments

This change conforms the rule to its federal counterpart. The federal rule was amended in 1993 to create a more usable mechanism for exchanging questions and submitting them to the witness. One goal of this change is to make depositions on written questions a more useful discovery device, recognizing that if it can be used effectively it has good potential for reducing the cost of litigation.

The amendment of this rule also serves the goal of facilitating the handling of these depositions by court reporters and others not regularly exposed to Minnesota practice.

31.03. Notice of Filing

When the deposition is received from the officer, the party taking it shall promptly give notice thereof to all other parties.

RULE 32. USE OF DEPOSITIONS IN COURT PROCEEDINGS

32.01. Use of Depositions

At the trial or upon the hearing of a motion or an interlocutory proceeding, any part or all of a deposition, so far as admissible under the Minnesota Rules of Evidence applied as though the witness were then present and testifying, and subject to the provisions of Rule 32.02, may be used against any party who was present or represented at the taking of the deposition or who had reasonable notice thereof in accordance with any one of the following provisions:

(a) Any deposition may be used by any party for the purpose of contradicting or impeaching the testimony of deponent as a witness or for any purpose permitted by the Minnesota Rules of Evidence.

(b) The deposition of a party or of any one who at the time of taking the deposition was an officer, director, employee, or managing agent or a person designated pursuant to Rules 30.02(f) or 31.01 to testify on behalf of a public or private corporation, partnership, association, or governmental agency which is a party may be used by an adverse party for any purpose.

(c) The deposition of a witness, whether or not a party, may be used by any party for any purpose if the court finds:
    (1) that the witness is dead; or
    (2) that the witness is at a greater distance than 100 miles from the place of trial or hearing, or is out of the state, unless it appears that the absence of the witness was procured by the party offering the deposition; or
    (3) that the witness is unable to attend or testify because of age, sickness, infirmity, or imprisonment; or
    (4) that the party offering the deposition has been unable to procure the attendance of the witness by subpoena; or
    (5) upon application and notice, that such exceptional circumstances exist as to make it desirable, in the interest of justice and with due regard to the importance of presenting the testimony of witness orally in open court, to allow the deposition to be used.

(d) If only part of a deposition is offered in evidence by a party, an adverse party may require the offering party to introduce any other part which ought in fairness to be considered with the part introduced and any party may introduce any other parts.

Substitution of parties pursuant to Rule 25 does not affect the right to use depositions previously taken; and, when an action has been brought in any court of the United States or any state and another action involving the same subject matter is afterward brought between the same parties or their representatives or successors in interest, all depositions lawfully taken and duly filed in the former action may be used in the latter as if originally taken therefor. A deposition previously taken may also be used as permitted by the Minnesota Rules of Evidence.

32.02. Objections to Admissibility

Subject to the provisions of Rules 28.02 and 32.04(c), objection may be made at the trial or hearing to receiving in evidence any deposition or part thereof for any reason which would require the exclusion of evidence if the witness were then present and testifying.

32.03. Form of Presentation

Except as otherwise directed by the court, a party offering deposition testimony pursuant to this rule may offer it in stenographic or nonstenographic form, but, if in nonstenographic form, the party shall also provide the court with a transcript of the portions so offered. On request of any party in a case tried before a jury, deposition testimony offered other than for impeachment purposes shall be presented in nonstenographic form, if available, unless the court for good cause orders otherwise.

(Amended effective January 1, 1997.)

Advisory Committee Comments--1996 Amendments

This change conforms the rule to its federal counterpart. As is true for the amendments to Rules 30 and 31, the committee believes it is advantageous to have great uniformity in practice in the area of deposition practice because of the likelihood that some of the players in many depositions are totally unfamiliar with Minnesota Procedure.

32.04. Effect of Errors and Irregularities in Depositions

(a) **As to Notice.** All errors and irregularities in the notice for taking a deposition are waived unless written objection is promptly served upon the party giving the notice.

(b) **As to Disqualification of Officer.** Objection to taking a deposition because of disqualification of the officer before whom it is to be taken is waived unless made before the taking of the deposition begins or as soon thereafter as the disqualification becomes known or could be discovered with reasonable diligence.

(c) **As to Taking of Deposition.**

(1) Objections to the competency of a witness or to the competency, relevancy, or materiality of testimony are not waived by failure to make them before or during the taking of the deposition, unless the ground of the objection is one which might have been obviated or removed if presented at that time.

(2) Errors and irregularities occurring at the oral examination in the manner of taking the deposition, in the form of the questions or answers, in the oath or affirmation, or in the conduct of parties, and errors of any kind which might be obviated, removed, or cured if promptly presented, are waived unless seasonable objection thereto is made at the taking of the deposition.

(3) Objections to the form of written questions submitted pursuant to Rule 31 are waived unless served in writing upon the party propounding them within the time allowed for serving the succeeding cross or other questions and within 7 days after service of the last questions authorized.

(d) **As to Completion and Return of Deposition.** Errors and irregularities in the manner in which the testimony is transcribed, preserved or the deposition is prepared, signed, certified, sealed, endorsed, transmitted, filed, or otherwise dealt with by the officer pursuant to Rules 30 and 31 are waived unless a motion to suppress the deposition or some part thereof is made with reasonable promptness after such defect is, or with due diligence might have been, ascertained.

(Amended effective January 1, 2020.)

32.05. Use of Video Depositions

Video depositions may be used in court proceedings to the same extent as stenographically recorded depositions.

(Amended effective July 1, 2015.)

Advisory Committee Comment—2020 Amendments

Rule 32.04(c)(3) is amended as part of the extensive amendments made to the timing provisions of the rules. These amendments implement the adoption of a standard "day" for counting deadlines under the rules—counting all days regardless of the length of the period and standardizing the time periods, where practicable, to a 7-, 14-, 21- or 28-day schedule. The only change to this rule lengthens the 5-day deadline for objections to the form of written questions to 7 days. This change affects only the time limit, and is not intended to have any other effect, and because weekend days and holidays are now included in the counting of days, the old 5-day period will most often be the same as the new 7-day period.

RULE 33. INTERROGATORIES TO PARTIES

33.01. Availability

(a) Any party may serve written interrogatories upon any other party. Interrogatories may, without leave of court, be served upon any party after service of the summons and complaint. No party may serve more than a total of 50 interrogatories upon any other party unless permitted to do so by the court upon motion, notice and a showing of good cause. In computing the total number of interrogatories each subdivision of separate questions shall be counted as an interrogatory.

(b) The party upon whom the interrogatories have been served shall serve separate written answers or objections to each interrogatory within 30 days after service of the interrogatories, except that a defendant may serve answers or objections within 45 days after service of summons and complaint upon that defendant. The court, on motion and notice and for good cause shown, may enlarge or shorten the time.

(c) Objections shall state with particularity the grounds for the objection and may be served either as a part of the document containing the answers or separately. The party submitting the interrogatories may move for an order under Rule 37.01 with respect to any objection to or other failure to answer an interrogatory. Answers to interrogatories to which objection has been made shall be deferred until the objections are determined.

(d) Answers to interrogatories shall be stated fully in writing and shall be signed under oath or penalty of perjury by the party served or, if the party served is the state, a corporation, a partnership, or an association, by any officer or managing agent, who shall furnish such information as is available. A party shall restate the interrogatory being answered immediately preceding the answer to that interrogatory.

All answers signed under penalty of perjury must have the signature affixed immediately below a declaration using substantially the following language: "I declare under penalty of perjury that everything I have stated in this document is true and correct." In addition to the signature, the date of signing and the county and state where the document was signed shall be noted on the document.

Without leave of court or written stipulation, any party may serve upon any other party written interrogatories, not exceeding 50 in number including all discrete subparts, to be answered by the party served or, if the party served is a public or private corporation or a partnership or association or governmental agency, by any officer or agent, who shall furnish such information as is available to the party. Leave to serve additional interrogatories shall be granted to the extent consistent with the principles of Rule 26.02(a).

(Amended effective July 1, 2015.)

Advisory Committee Comments--1996 Amendments

This change retains the existing rule on interrogatories, and does not adopt the 1993 amendment to its federal counterpart. The federal courts adopted in 1993 an express numerical limitation on the number of interrogatories, limiting them to 25. Minnesota took this action to limit discovery in the 1975 amendments to the rules, limiting interrogatories to 50, and this limit has worked well in practice. The committee believes that the other changes in the federal rules are not significant enough in substance to warrant adoption in Minnesota.

The rule, however, is amended in one important way. The existing provision requiring a party receiving objections to interrogatories to move within 15 days to have the objections determined by the court and the waiver of a right to answers if such a motion is not made within the required time has not worked well. There is no reason to require such prompt action, and much to commend more orderly consideration of the objections. The absolute waiver of the old rule gives way to an explicit right to have the matter resolved by the court, and permits that to be done at any time. This permits the party receiving objections to determine their validity, attempt to resolve any dispute, consider the eventual importance of the information, and possibly to take the matter up with the court in conjunction with other matters. All of these reasons favor a more flexible rule.

Advisory Committee Comments—2015 Amendments

Rule 33.01 is amended to implement a new statute directing the courts to accept documents without notarization if they are signed under the following language: "I declare under penalty of perjury that everything I have stated in this document is true and correct." Minn. Stat. § 358.116 (2014) (codifying 2014 Minn. Laws ch. 204, § 3). The statute allows the courts to require specifically by rule that notarization is necessary, but the difficulty in accomplishing and documenting notarization for documents that are e-filed and e-served militates against requiring formal notarization. Accordingly, interrogatory answers may be signed by the party under penalty of perjury, so long as the appropriate language is included above the party's signature. The rule also requires inclusion of the date of signing and the county and state where signed to provide information necessary to establish the fact and venue of possible perjury; this information is otherwise provided by notarization. Rule 15 of the Minnesota General Rules of Practice establishes uniform requirements for the formalities of documents signed under penalty of perjury.

33.02. Scope; Use at Trial

Interrogatories may relate to any matters which can be inquired into pursuant to Rule 26.02, and the answers may be used to the extent permitted by the Minnesota Rules of Evidence.

An interrogatory otherwise proper is not necessarily objectionable merely because its answer involves an opinion or contention that relates to fact or the application of law to fact, but the court may order that such an interrogatory need not be answered until after designated discovery has been completed, a pretrial conference has been held, or at another later time.

33.03. Option to Produce Business Records

Where the answer to an interrogatory may be derived or ascertained from the business records, including electronically stored information, of the party upon whom the interrogatory has been served or from an examination, audit, or inspection of such business records, including a compilation, abstract, or summary thereof, and the burden of deriving or ascertaining the answer is substantially the same for the party serving the interrogatory as for the party served, it is a sufficient answer to such interrogatory to specify the records from which the answer may be derived or ascertained and to afford to the party serving the interrogatory reasonable opportunity to examine, audit, or inspect such records and to make copies, compilations, abstracts, or summaries. A specification shall be in sufficient detail as to permit the interrogating party to locate and to identify, as readily as can the party served, the records from which the answer may be ascertained.

(Amended effective July 1, 2007.)

Advisory Committee Comment—2007 Amendment

The amendment to Rule 33.03 in 2007 is simple but important. The existing rule allows a party to respond to an interrogatory by directing the requesting party to discover the information from designated documents. The amended rule does not change this procedure, but simply allows the responding party to designate electronic records from which the requested information can be obtained.

RULE 34. PRODUCTION OF DOCUMENTS, ELECTRONICALLY STORED INFORMATION, AND THINGS AND ENTRY UPON LAND FOR INSPECTION AND OTHER PURPOSES

34.01. Scope

(a) In General. Any party may serve on any other party a request within the scope of Rule 26.02:

(1) to produce and permit the party making the request, or someone acting on the requesting party's behalf, to inspect and copy, test, or sample:

(A) any designated documents or electronically stored information—including writings, drawings, graphs, charts, photographs, sound recordings, images, and other data or data compilations stored in any medium from which information can be obtained—translated, if necessary—by the respondent through detection devices into reasonably usable form, or (B) to inspect and copy, test, or sample any designated tangible things that constitute or contain matters within the scope of Rule 26.02 and that are in the possession, custody or control of the party upon whom the request is served, or

(2) to permit entry upon designated land or other property in the possession or control of the party upon whom the request is served for the purpose of inspection and measuring, surveying, photographing, testing, or sampling the property or any designated object or operation thereon, within the scope of Rule 26.02.

(Amended effective July 1, 2018.)

Advisory Committee Comment—2007 Amendment

Rule 34.01 is amended to make two changes. First, the rule explicitly applies to "electronically stored information" ("ESI") as well as other forms. A more important change is to add provisions allowing the discovering party to require production of information for the purposes of testing or sampling. Testing and sampling are important tools in managing discovery, particularly discovery of ESI. Testing and sampling allow a party to inspect a small subset of requested information to determine whether it is worth conducting additional or broader discovery. These tools may be useful to the court in determining whether to allow additional discovery or discovery of information that is not reasonably accessible, as defined in Rule 26.02(b)(2).

Advisory Committee Comment—2018 Amendments

Rule 34.01 is amended to incorporate the scope of discovery set forth in Rule 26.02. This change is made to make that limitation on the scope of any Rule 34 discovery obligation clear to litigants, and is not intended to expand or narrow the scope of discovery.

34.02. Procedure

(a) **Timing.** The request may, without leave of court, be served upon any party with or after service of the summons and complaint.

(b) **Contents of the Request.** The request:
(1) must set forth with reasonable particularity each item or category of items to be inspected;
(2) must specify a reasonable time, place, and manner for the inspection and performing the related acts.; and
(3) may specify the form or forms in which electronically stored information is to be produced.

(c) **Responses and Objections**.
(1) **Time to Respond**. The party upon whom the request is served must serve a written response within 30 days after the party is served (or deemed served pursuant to Rule 26.04(b)). The court may allow a shorter or longer time.

(2) **Responding to Each Item.** The response shall state, with respect to each item or category, either that inspection and related activities will be permitted as requested, or state with specificity the grounds for objecting to the request, including the reasons. The responding party may state that it will produce copies of documents or of electronically stored information instead of permitting inspection. The production must then be completed no later than the time for inspection specified in the request or another reasonable time specified in the response.

(3) **Objections.** An objection must state whether any responsive materials are being withheld on the basis of that objection. If objection is made to part of an item or category, that part shall be specified and inspection permitted of the remaining parts.

(4) **Responding to a Request for Production of Electronically Stored Information.** The response may state an objection to a requested form for producing electronically stored information. If no form was specified in the request, the responding party must state the form or forms it intends to use.

(5) **Producing the Documents or Electronically Stored Information.**–Unless otherwise stipulated or ordered by the court, these procedures apply to producing documents and electronically stored information:

(A) A party must produce documents as they are kept in the usual course of business at the time of the request and may organize them to correspond to the categories in the request;

(B) If a request does not specify the form for producing electronically stored information, a responding party must produce the information in a form or forms in which it is ordinarily maintained or in a reasonably usable form; and

(C) A party need not produce the same electronically stored information in more than one form.

(Amended effective July 1, 2018.)

Advisory Committee Comment—2007 Amendment

Rule 34.02 is amended to establish presumptive rules for the procedural aspects of discovery of electrically stored information. These include allowing the party seeking discovery to specify the form or medium for response, providing a default rule that applies if the request does not specify a form, and making it clear that a party does not need to produce information in more than one form.

Advisory Committee Comment—2018 Amendments

Rule 34.02 is amended to adopt the changes made to Federal Rule 34 in 2015. The most significant change is the provision in Rule 34.02(c)(3) that requires a party asserting an objection to a request for production to disclose whether any document is being withheld from production based on those objections. This rule change has curtailed one aspect of game-playing from federal practice and has worked well in federal court. It is adopted in state court practice to accomplish the same purpose. The rule does not require a detailed log of all documents withheld, but the objecting party must make it clear that documents are being withheld based on the objections asserted. This disclosure can then support dialogue over the nature of withheld information and a motion to resolve the appropriateness of the objections asserted.

The rule is also reformatted to make it clearer and easier to use by adding subdivisions and headings. These formatting changes are not intended to affect the interpretation of the rule.

34.03. Persons Not Parties

(a) Subpoenas. As provided in Rule 45, a nonparty may be compelled to produce documents and electronically stored information and to permit an inspection.

(b) Independent Actions. This rule does not preclude an independent action against a person not a party for production of documents and things and permission to enter upon land.

Advisory Committee Comment—2018 Amendments

Rule 34.03(a) is a new section that makes clear that Rule 34 requests may be enforced against nonparties through use of subpoenas issued pursuant to Rule 45.

RULE 35. PHYSICAL, MENTAL, AND BLOOD EXAMINATION OF PERSONS

35.01. Order of Examinations

In an action in which the physical or mental condition or the blood relationship of a party, or of an agent of a party, or of a person under control of a party, is in controversy, the court in which the action is pending may order the party to submit to, or produce such agent or person for a physical, mental, or blood examination by a suitably licensed or certified examiner. The order may be made only on motion for good cause shown and upon notice to the party or person to be examined and to all other parties and shall specify the time, place, manner, conditions, and scope of the examination and the person or persons by whom it is made.

(Amended effective March 1, 1994.)

35.02. Report of Findings

(a) If requested by the party against whom an order is made pursuant to Rule 35.01 or by the person examined, the party causing the examination to be made shall deliver to the requesting party a copy of a detailed written report of the examination setting out the examiner's findings and conclusions, together with like reports of all earlier examinations of the same condition. After such request and delivery, the party causing the examination to be made shall be entitled, upon request, to receive from the party or person examined a like report of any examination, previously or thereafter made, of the same physical, mental, or blood condition. If the party or person examined refuses to deliver such report, the court, on motion and notice, may make an order requiring delivery on such terms as are just, and, if an examiner fails or refuses to make such a report, the court may exclude the examiner's testimony if offered at the trial.

(b) By requesting and obtaining a report of the examination so ordered or by taking the deposition of the examiner, the adverse party waives any privilege the party may have in that action or any other involving the same controversy, regarding the testimony of every other person who has examined or may thereafter examine the party or the person under the party's control with respect to the same physical, mental, or blood condition.

(Amended effective March 1, 1994.)

35.03. Waiver of Medical Privilege

If at any stage of an action a party voluntarily places in controversy the physical, mental, or blood condition of that party, a decedent, or a person under that party's control, such party thereby waives any privilege that party may have in that action regarding the testimony of every person who has examined or may thereafter examine that party or the person under that party's control with respect to the same physical, mental, or blood condition.

35.04. Medical Disclosures and Depositions of Medical Experts

When a party has waived medical privilege pursuant to Rule 35.03, such party within 14 days of a written request by any other party,
(a) shall furnish to the requesting party copies of all medical reports previously or thereafter made by any treating or examining medical expert, and
(b) shall provide written authority signed by the party of whom request is made to permit the inspection of all hospital and other medical records, concerning the physical, mental, or blood condition of such party as to which privilege has been waived.

Disclosures pursuant to this rule shall include the conclusions of such treating or examining medical expert.

Depositions of treating or examining medical experts shall not be taken except upon order of the court for good cause shown upon motion and notice to the parties and upon such terms as the court may provide.

(Amended effective January 1, 2020.)

Advisory Committee Comment--1993 Amendments

The amendments to Rule 35 are intended to expand the power of the courts to order examinations by professionals other than physicians. This amendment is generally consistent with amendments made to Fed. R. Civ. P. 35 in 1991, though the state and federal rules have always been somewhat different.

This amendment recognizes that examination may be appropriate by, for example, a licensed psychologist, dentist, audiologist, or physical or occupational therapist. These licensed professionals are not physicians but may, and often do, provide valuable information or testimony. See Fed. R. Civ. P. 35, Notes of Advisory Committee--1991 Amendment, reprinted in Federal Civil Judicial Procedure & Rules 126 (West pamph. 1993).

Advisory Committee Comment—2020 Amendments

Rule 35.04 is amended as part of the extensive amendments made to the timing provisions of the rules. These amendments implement the adoption of a standard "day" for counting deadlines under the rules—counting all days regardless of the length of the period and standardizing the time periods, where practicable, to a 7-, 14-, 21- or 28-day schedule. The only change to this rule lengthens the 10-day period to respond to written requests to a 14-day period. This change affects only the time limits, and is not intended to have any other effect.

RULE 36. REQUESTS FOR ADMISSION

36.01. Request for Admission

A party may serve upon any other party a written request for the admission, for purposes of the pending action only, of the truth of any matters within the scope of Rule 26.02 set forth in the request that relate to statements, opinions of fact, or the application of law to fact, including the genuineness of any documents described in the request. Copies of documents shall be served with the request, unless they have been or are otherwise furnished or made available for inspection and copying. The request may, without leave of court, be served after service of the summons and complaint.

Each matter of which an admission is requested shall be separately set forth. The matter is admitted unless within 30 days after service of the request, or within such shorter or longer time as the court may allow, the party to whom the request is directed serves upon the party requesting the admission a written answer or objection addressed to the matter, signed by the party or by the party's attorney; but, unless the court shortens the time, a defendant shall not be required to serve answers or objections before the expiration of 45 days after service of the summons and complaint upon that defendant. If objection is made, the reasons therefor shall be stated. The answer shall specifically deny the matter or set forth in detail the reasons why the answering party cannot truthfully admit or deny the matter. A denial shall fairly meet the substance of the requested admission, and, when good faith requires that a party qualify an answer or deny only a part of the matter of which an admission is requested, the party shall specify so much of it as is true and qualify or deny the remainder. An answering party may not give lack of information or knowledge as a reason for failure to admit or deny unless the party states that a reasonable inquiry has been made and that the information known or readily obtainable by the party is insufficient to enable the party to admit or deny. A party who considers that a matter of which an admission has been requested presents a genuine issue for trial may not, on that ground alone, object to the request; the party may, subject to the provisions of Rule 37.03, deny the matter or set forth reasons why the party cannot admit or deny it.

The party who has requested the admissions may move to determine the sufficiency of the answers or objections. Unless the court determines that an objection is justified, it shall order that an answer be served. If the court determines that an answer does not comply with the requirements of this rule, it may order either that the matter is admitted or that an amended answer be served. The court may, in lieu of these orders, determine that final disposition of the request is to be made at a pretrial conference or at a designated time prior to trial. The provisions of Rule 37.01(d) apply to the award of expenses incurred in connection with the motion.

36.02. Effect of Admission

Any matter admitted pursuant to this rule is conclusively established unless the court on motion permits withdrawal or amendment of the admission. Subject to Rule 16 governing amendment of a pretrial order, the court may permit withdrawal or amendment when the presentation of the merits of the action will be subserved thereby and the party who obtained the admission fails to satisfy the court that withdrawal or amendment will prejudice that party in maintaining the action or defense on the merits. Any admission made by a party hereunder is for the purpose of the pending action only and is not an admission by that party for any other purpose nor may it be used against that party in any other proceeding.

RULE 37. FAILURE TO MAKE DISCLOSURES OR TO COOPERATE IN DISCOVERY: SANCTIONS

37.01. Motion for Order Compelling Disclosure or Discovery

(a) **Appropriate Court.** An application for an order to a party shall be made to the court in which the action is pending. An application for an order to a person who is not a party shall be made to the court in the county where the discovery is being, or is to be, taken.

(b) **Specific Motions.**

    (1) To Compel Disclosure. If a party fails to make a disclosure required by Rule 26.01, any other party may move to compel disclosure and for appropriate sanctions.

    (2) To Compel a Discovery Response. A party seeking discovery may move for an order compelling an answer, designation, production, or inspection. This motion may be made if:

        (A) a deponent fails to answer a question propounded or submitted under Rules 30 or 31;

        (B) a corporation or other entity fails to make a designation under Rule 30.02(f) or 31.01(c);

        (C) a party fails to answer an interrogatory submitted under Rule 33; or

        (D) a party fails to produce documents or fails to respond that inspection will be permitted—or fails to permit inspection—as requested under Rule 34.

The motion must include a certification that the movant has in good faith conferred or attempted to confer with the person or party failing to make the discovery in an effort to secure the information or material without court action. When taking a deposition on oral examination, the proponent of the question may complete or adjourn the examination before applying for an order.

(c) **Evasive or Incomplete Answer, or Response.** For purposes of this subdivision an evasive or incomplete disclosure, answer, or response is to be treated as a failure to disclose, answer, or respond.

(d) **Expenses and Sanctions.**

(1) If the motion is granted, or if the requested discovery is provided after the motion was filed, the court shall, after affording an opportunity to be heard, require the party or deponent whose conduct necessitated the motion or the party or attorney advising such conduct or both of them to pay to the moving party the reasonable expenses incurred in making the motion, including attorney fees, unless the court finds that the motion was filed without the movant's first making a good faith effort to obtain the discovery without court action, or that the opposing party's nondisclosure, response, or objection was substantially justified or that other circumstances make an award of expenses unjust.

(2) If the motion is denied, the court may enter any protective order authorized under Rule 26.03 and shall, after affording an opportunity to be heard, require the moving party or the attorney filing the motion or both of them to pay to the party or deponent who opposed the motion the reasonable expenses incurred in opposing the motion, including attorney fees, unless the court finds that the making of the motion was substantially justified or that other circumstances make an award of expenses unjust.

(3) If the motion is granted in part and denied in part, the court may enter any protective order authorized under Rule 26.03 and may, after affording an opportunity to be heard, apportion the reasonable expenses incurred in relation to the motion among the parties and persons in a just manner.

(Amended effective July 1, 2018.)

Advisory Committee Comments--1996 Amendments

This change conforms the rule to its federal counterpart, consistent with the ongoing differences between the two rules.

Advisory Committee Comment—2018 Amendments

Rule 37 is amended to adopt changes made to Federal Rule 37 in 2015. Rule 37.01(b)(2)(D) is amended to provide express authority for a motion for an order compelling discovery when a party fails to respond to a request either by the production of requested information or by the agreement to permit inspection. This amendment provides the means for enforcing the obligations under amended Rule 34.02.

37.02. Failure to Comply with Order

    (a)   **Sanctions by Court in County Where Deposition is Taken.** If a deponent fails to be sworn or to answer a question after being directed to do so by the court in the county in which the deposition is being taken, the failure may be considered a contempt of that court.

    (b)   **Sanctions by Court in Which Action is Pending.** If a party or an officer, director, employee, or managing agent of a party or a person designated in Rule 30.02(f) or 31.01 to testify on behalf of a party fails to obey an order to provide or permit discovery, including an order made pursuant to Rule 35 or 37.01, the court in which the action is pending may make such orders in regard to the failure as are just, and among others the following:

        (1)   An order that the matters regarding which the order was made or any other designated facts shall be taken to be established for the purposes of the action in accordance with the claim of the party obtaining the order;

        (2)   An order refusing to allow the disobedient party to support or oppose designated claims or defenses, or prohibiting that party from introducing designated matters in evidence;

        (3)   An order striking pleadings or parts thereof, staying further proceedings until the order is obeyed, dismissing the action or proceeding or any part thereof, or rendering a judgment by default against the disobedient party;

        (4)   In lieu of any of the foregoing orders or in addition thereto, an order treating as a contempt of court the failure to obey any orders except an order to submit to a physical or mental examination;

        (5)   Where a party has failed to comply with an order pursuant to Rule 35.01 requiring that party to produce another for examination, such orders as are listed herein in paragraphs (1), (2), and (3), unless the party failing to comply shows that that party is unable to produce such person for examination.

    In lieu of any of the foregoing orders or in addition thereto, the court shall require the party failing to obey the order or the attorney advising that party or both to pay the reasonable expenses, including attorney fees, caused by the failure, unless the court finds that the failure was substantially justified or that other circumstances make an award of expenses unjust.

37.03. Failure to Disclose, to Supplement an Earlier Response or to Admit

    (a)   **Failure to Disclose or Supplement.** If a party fails to provide information or identify a witness as required by Rule 26.01 or .05, the party is not allowed to use that information or witness to supply evidence on a motion, at a hearing, or at a trial, unless the failure was substantially justified or is harmless. In addition to or instead of this sanction, the court, on motion and after giving an opportunity to be heard:

(1) may order payment of the reasonable expenses, including attorney's fees, caused by the failure;

(2) may inform the jury of the party's failure; and

(3) may impose other appropriate sanctions, including any of the orders listed in Rule 37.02.

(b) **Failure to Admit.** If a party fails to admit the genuineness of any documents or the truth of any matter as requested pursuant to Rule 36, and if the party requesting the admissions thereafter proves the genuineness of the document or the truth of any such matter, the requesting party may apply to the court for an order requiring the other party to pay the reasonable expenses incurred in making that proof, including reasonable attorney fees. The court shall make the order unless it finds that (1) the request was held objectionable pursuant to Rule 36.01, or (2) the admission sought was of no substantial importance, or (3) the party failing to admit had reasonable ground to believe that the party might prevail on the matter, or (4) there was other good reason for the failure to admit.

(Amended effective July 1, 2013.)

37.04. Failure of a Party to Attend at Own Deposition or Serve Answers

If a party or an officer, director, employee, or managing agent of a party or a person designated in Rule 30.02(f) or 31.01 to testify on behalf of a party fails (1) to appear before the officer who is to take the deposition, after being served with a proper notice, or (2) to serve answers or objections to interrogatories submitted pursuant to Rule 33, after proper service of the interrogatories, or (3) to serve a written response to a request for inspection submitted pursuant to Rule 34, after proper service of the request, the court in which the action is pending on motion may make such orders in regard to the failure as are just, including any action authorized in Rule 37.02(b)(1), (2), and (3). In lieu of any order or in addition thereto, the court shall require the party failing to act or the attorney advising that party or both to pay the reasonable expenses, including attorney fees, caused by the failure, unless the court finds that the failure was substantially justified or that other circumstances make an award of expenses unjust.

The failure to act described herein may not be excused on the ground that the discovery sought is objectionable unless the party failing to act has applied for a protective order as provided by Rule 26.03.

37.05. Failure to Preserve Electronically Stored Information

If electronically stored information that should have been preserved in the anticipation or conduct of litigation is lost because a party failed to take reasonable steps to preserve it, and it cannot be restored or replaced through additional discovery, the court:
(a) upon finding prejudice to another party from loss of the information, may order measures no greater than necessary to cure the prejudice; or
(b) only upon finding that the party acted with the intent to deprive another party of the information's use in the litigation may:

(1) presume that the lost information was unfavorable to the party;
(2) instruct the jury that it may or must presume the information was unfavorable to the party; or
(3) dismiss the action or enter a default judgment.

(Adopted effective July 1, 2018.)

Advisory Committee Comment—2007 Amendment

Rule 37.05 is a new rule; it is identical to Fed. R. Civ. P. 37(f), adopted in 2006. It provides some protection against the automatic imposition of sanctions that might otherwise be required under the rules. This rule applies only to discovery of electronically stored information, and prevents the imposition of sanctions for spoliation of evidence where the loss of information arises from the routine operation of a computer system. The good-faith part of this test is important and is not met if a party fails to take appropriate steps to preserve data once a duty to preserve arises.

Advisory Committee Comment—2018 Amendments

Rule 37.05 is amended to redefine the sanctions available for the failure to preserve electronically stored information ("ESI"). The amendment follows closely the amendment made to Fed. R. Civ. P. 37(e) in 2015 and is intended to create a clearer standard for imposition of sanctions for the failure to preserve electronically stored information. First, the rule looks to ameliorating any prejudice by allowing discovery to restore or replace the missing information. This might be accomplished by locating alternate copies of the information, or reconstructing backed up copies. In the absence of prejudice, the rule does not authorize the imposition of sanctions for loss of information. The rule does not limit other sanctions based on conduct other than failure to preserve ESI. If prejudice does occur, the amended rule requires that a remedial sanction be implemented—one that is designed and limited to curing the prejudice. Most often, this would be an order precluding evidence or limiting claims or defenses affected by the missing ESI. If the missing ESI was intentionally destroyed or otherwise made unavailable, the rule allows the more drastic sanctions of imposition of a presumption or either allowing or requiring a jury either to draw an adverse inference that the information was unfavorable to the party or, in egregious situations, dismiss the action or grant a default judgment.

By its terms, this rule applies only to failure to produce ESI where there is a duty to preserve it. There is no reason, however, that the courts should not, in the exercise of their discretion, follow this rule where there is the failure to preserve other evidence, such as physical evidence or documents in non-electronic form.

37.06. Failure to Participate in Framing a Discovery Plan

If a party or its attorney fails to participate in good faith in developing and submitting a proposed discovery plan as required by Rule 26.06, the court may, after giving an opportunity to be heard, require that party or attorney to pay to any other party the reasonable expenses, including attorney's fees, caused by the failure.

(Adopted effective July 1, 2013.)

VI. TRIALS

RULE 38. JURY TRIAL OF RIGHT

38.01. Right Preserved

In actions for the recovery of money only, or of specific real or personal property, the issues of fact shall be tried by a jury, unless a jury trial is waived or a reference is ordered.

38.02. Waiver

In actions arising on contract, and by permission of the court in other actions, any party thereto may waive a jury trial by:
- (a) failing to appear at the trial;
- (b) written consent, by the party or the party's attorney, filed with the court administrator; or
- (c) oral consent in open court, entered in the minutes.

Neither the failure to file any document requesting a jury trial nor the failure to pay a jury fee shall be deemed a waiver of the right to a jury trial.

(Amended effective March 1, 1994.)

Advisory Committee Comment--1993 Amendments

The committee is of the opinion that waiver of the right to a jury trial should not be found from inaction or failure to pay a jury fee. The amendment, coupled with the abolition of the note of issue, should obviate any confusion or inadvertent waiver of the constitutionality protected right to a jury trial. See Schweich v. Ziegler, Inc., 463 N.W.2d 722 (Minn. 1991).

38.03. Placing Action on Calendar

Rule 38.03 is repealed, effective January 1, 1992.

Task Force Comment--1991 Adoption

This amendment to repeal this rule is appropriate because the use of notes of issue filed by the parties will be replaced by the court-initiated scheduling. See proposed Minn. Gen. R. Prac. 111.

RULE 39. TRIAL BY JURY OR BY THE COURT

39.01. By Court

Issues of fact not submitted to a jury as provided in Rule 38 shall be tried by the court.

39.02. Advisory Jury and Trial by Consent

In all actions not triable of right by a jury, the court, upon motion or upon its own initiative, may try an issue with an advisory jury, or the court, with the consent of both parties, may order a trial with a jury whose verdict has the same effect as if trial by jury had been a matter of right.

39.03. Preliminary Instructions in Jury Trials

After the jury has been impaneled and sworn, and before opening statements of counsel, the court may instruct the jury as to the respective claims of the parties and as to such other matters as will aid the jury in comprehending the trial procedure and sequence to be followed. Preliminary instructions may also embrace such matters as burden of proof and preponderance of evidence, the elements which the jury may consider in weighing testimony or determining credibility of witnesses, rules applicable to opinion evidence, and such other rules of law as the court may deem essential to the proper understanding of the evidence.

39.04. Opening Statements by Counsel

Before any evidence is introduced, plaintiff may make an opening statement, whereupon any other party may make an opening statement or may reserve the same until that party's case in chief is opened. Opening statements may be waived by any party to the action without affecting the right of any other party to make such an opening statement.

RULE 40. ASSIGNMENT OF CASES FOR TRIAL

The judges of the court may, by order or by rule of court, provide for the setting of cases for trial upon the calendar, the order in which they shall be heard, and the resetting thereof.

RULE 41. DISMISSAL OF ACTIONS

41.01. Voluntary Dismissal; Effect Thereof

(a) **By Plaintiff by Stipulation.** Subject to the provisions of Rules 23.05, 23.09 and 66, an action may be dismissed by the plaintiff without order of court (1) by filing a notice of dismissal at any time before service by the adverse party of an answer or of a motion for summary judgment, whichever first occurs, or (2) by filing a stipulation of dismissal signed by all parties who have appeared in the action. Unless otherwise stated in the notice of dismissal or stipulation, the dismissal is without prejudice, except that a notice of dismissal operates as an adjudication upon the merits when filed by a plaintiff who has once dismissed in any court of the United States or of any state an action based on or including the same claim.

(b) **By Order of Court.** Except as provided in clause (a) of this rule, an action shall not be dismissed at the plaintiff's instance except upon order of the court and upon such terms and conditions as the court deems proper. If a counterclaim has been pleaded by a defendant prior to the service upon the defendant of the plaintiff's motion to dismiss, the action shall not be dismissed against the defendant's objection unless the counterclaim may remain pending for independent adjudication by the court. Unless otherwise specified in the order, a dismissal herein is without prejudice.

(Amended effective January 1, 2006.)

Advisory Committee Comment--1993 Amendments

The amendment to this rule is made to conform the rule to its counterpart in the Federal Rules of Civil Procedure, Fed. R. Civ. P. 41(a)(1). The existing rule in Minnesota seems to the committee archaic, establishing time requirements on the commencement of terms of court. Since 1977, Minnesota trial courts have had continuous terms. Minnesota Statutes, section 484.08 (1992).

The former rule has permitted parties to dismiss claims without prejudice even after extensive discovery or other pretrial proceedings have taken place. Dismissal without prejudice has also been possible after the trial court has issued orders on preliminary matters. The right to dismiss on the eve of trial has prejudiced defendants or has required courts to consider motions to deny a plaintiff the right to dismiss without prejudice. The committee is of the opinion that the right to dismiss without prejudice ought to be limited to a fairly short period after commencement of the action when prejudice to opponents is likely to be minimal. The Advisory Committee considered recommending a change to Rule 53 to make express provision for the use of referees in alternative dispute resolution and settlement proceedings, but has concluded that amendment of the rule is not necessary inasmuch as the rule now permits use of referees for this purpose in limited appropriate circumstances. The Advisory Committee is also mindful that the Minnesota Supreme Court Alternative Dispute Resolution Implementation Committee has recently submitted its Final Report dated August 25, 1993. The Advisory Committee is of the opinion that that Report can be considered independently of the recommendations of this committee. The committee also believes that if more specific and comprehensive rules on the use of referees in alternative dispute resolution are advisable, such rules might better be incorporated in Rules for Alternative Dispute Resolution.

Advisory Committee Comment—2006 Amendment

Rule 41.01(a) is amended to renumber one of the rule cross-references to reflect the amendment and renumbering of Rule 23 as part of the amendments effective January 1, 2006.

41.02. Involuntary Dismissal; Effect Thereof

(a) The court may upon its own initiative, or upon motion of a party, and upon such notice as it may prescribe, dismiss an action or claim for failure to prosecute or to comply with these rules or any order of the court.

(b) After the plaintiff has completed the presentation of evidence, the defendant, without waiving the right to offer evidence in the event the motion is not granted, may move for a dismissal on the ground that upon the facts and the law, the plaintiff has shown no right to relief. In an action tried by the court without a jury, the court as trier of the fact may then determine the facts and render judgment against the plaintiff or may decline to render any judgment until the close of all the evidence. If the court renders judgment on the merits against the plaintiff, the court shall make findings as provided in Rule 52.01.

(c) Unless the court specifies otherwise in its order, a dismissal pursuant to this rule and any dismissal not provided for in this rule or in Rule 41.01, other than a dismissal for lack of jurisdiction, for forum non conveniens, or for failure to join a party indispensable pursuant to Rule 19, operates as an adjudication upon the merits.

41.03. Dismissal of Counterclaim, Cross-Claim, or Third-Party Claim

The provisions of Rules 41.01 and 41.02 apply to the dismissal of any counterclaim, cross-claim, or third-party claim.

41.04. Costs of Previously Dismissed Action

If a plaintiff who has once dismissed an action in any court commences an action based upon or including the same claim against the same defendant, the court may make such order for the payment of costs of the action previously dismissed as it may deem proper and may stay the proceedings in the action until the plaintiff has complied with the order.

RULE 42. SEPARATE TRIALS

42.01. Consolidation

When actions involving a common question of law or fact are pending before the court, it may order a joint hearing or trial of any or all the matters in issue in the actions; it may order all the actions consolidated; and it may make such orders concerning proceedings therein as may tend to avoid unnecessary costs or delay.

42.02. Separate Trials

The court, in furtherance of convenience or to avoid prejudice, or when separate trials will be conducive to expedition and economy, may order a separate trial of one or any number of claims, cross-claims, counterclaims, or third-party claims, or of any separate issues.

RULE 43. TAKING OF TESTIMONY

43.01. Form

In all trials the testimony of witnesses shall be taken orally in open court, unless otherwise provided by statute or by these rules, the Minnesota Rules of Evidence, or other rules adopted by the Supreme Court.

(Amended effective January 1, 1997.)

43.02.

(Abrogated effective January 1, 1997.)

43.03.

(Abrogated effective January 1, 1997.)

43.04. Affirmation in Lieu of Oath

Whenever under these rules an oath is required to be taken, a solemn affirmation may be accepted in lieu thereof.

43.05. Evidence and Motions

Whenever a motion is based on facts not appearing of record, the court may hear the matter on affidavits presented by the respective parties, but the court may direct that the matter be heard wholly or partly on oral testimony or depositions.

43.06.

(Abrogated effective January 1, 1997.)

43.07. Interpreters

The court may appoint an interpreter of its own selection and may fix reasonable compensation. The compensation shall be paid out of funds provided by law.

Advisory Committee Comments--1996 Amendments

The changes to this rule conforms it to its federal counterpart. The existing rule predates the adoption of the Minnesota Rules of Evidence, and creates conflicts with those rules in practice. It is appropriate to have all provisions relating to evidence contained in a single location, and to have the rules of civil procedure only refer to those rules where necessary.

Advisory Committee Comment—2006 Amendment

Rule 43.07 is amended to conform the rule to the statutory requirement that the "fees and expenses of a qualified per diem interpreter for a court must be paid by the state courts." Minn. Stat. § 546.44, subd. 3 (2004). Language is stricken from the second sentence to eliminate the conflict between the rule and statute regarding payment of court-appointed interpreters.

This amendment is drawn from the language of Minn. R. Crim. P. 26.03, subd. 16.

RULE 44. PROOF OF OFFICIAL RECORD

44.01. Authentication

(a) **Domestic.** An official record kept within the United States, or any state, district, commonwealth, or within a territory subject to the administrative or judicial jurisdiction of the United States, or an entry therein, when admissible for any purpose, may be evidenced by an official publication thereof or by a copy attested by the officer having the legal custody of the record, or by the officer's deputy, and accompanied by a certificate that such officer has the custody. The certificate may be made by a judge of a court of record of the district or political subdivision in which the record is kept, authenticated by the seal of the court, or may be made by any public officer having a seal of office and having official duties in the district or political subdivision in which the record is kept, authenticated by the seal of the officer's office.

(b) **Foreign.** A foreign official record, or an entry therein, when admissible for any purpose, may be evidenced by an official publication thereof; or a copy thereof, attested by a person authorized to make the attestation, and accompanied by a final certification as to the genuineness of the signature and official position (i) of the attesting person, or (ii) of any foreign official whose certificate of genuineness of signature and official position relates to the attestation or is in a chain of certificates of genuineness of signature and official position relating to the attestation. A final certification may be made by a secretary of embassy or legation, consul general, vice consul, or consular agent of the United States, or a diplomatic or consular official of the foreign country assigned or accredited to the United States. If reasonable opportunity has been given to all parties to investigate the authenticity and accuracy of the documents, the court may, for good cause shown, (i) admit an attested copy without final certification or (ii) permit the foreign official record to be evidenced by an attested summary with or without a final certification. The final certification is unnecessary if the record and the attestation are certified as provided in a treaty or convention to which the United States and the foreign country in which the official record is located are parties.

(Amended effective January 1, 1997.)

44.02. Lack of Record

A written statement that after diligent search no record or entry of a specified tenor is found to exist in the records designated by the statement, authenticated as provided in Rule 44.01(a) in the case of a domestic record, or complying with the requirements of Rule 44.01(b) for a summary in the case of a foreign record, is admissible as evidence that the records contain no such record or entry.

44.03. Other Proof

This rule does not prevent the proof of official records or of entry or lack of entry therein by any other method authorized by law.

44.04.

(Abrogated effective January 1, 1997.)

Advisory Committee Comments--1996 Amendments

These changes conform the rule to its federal counterpart. These amendments reflect the view that questions of evidence should be determined under the Minnesota Rules of Evidence and the decisional law arising under those rules. The existing rule is not helpful to courts or litigants.

RULE 45. SUBPOENA

45.01. Form; Issuance

(a) **Form.** Every subpoena shall
- (1) state the name of the court from which it is issued; and
- (2) state the title of the action, the name of the court in which it is pending, and its court file number, if one has been assigned; and
- (3) command each person to whom it is directed to attend and give testimony or to produce and permit inspection, copying, testing, or sampling of designated books, documents, electronically stored information, or tangible things in the possession, custody or control of that person, or to permit inspection of premises, at a time and place therein specified; and
- (4) contain a notice to the person to whom it is directed advising that person of the right to reimbursement for certain expenses pursuant to Rule 45.03(d), and the right to have the amount of those expenses determined prior to compliance with the subpoena.

A command to produce evidence or to permit inspection, copying, testing, or sampling may be joined with a command to appear at trial or hearing or at deposition, or may be issued separately. A subpoena may specify the form or forms in which electronically stored information is to be produced.

(b) **Subpoenas Issued In Name of Court.** A subpoena commanding attendance at a trial or hearing, for attendance at a deposition, or for production or inspection, copying, testing, or sampling shall be issued in the name of the court where the action is pending.

(c) **Issuance by Court or by Attorney.** The court administrator shall issue a subpoena, signed but otherwise in blank, to a party requesting it, who shall complete it before service. An attorney as officer of the court may also issue and sign a subpoena on behalf of the court where the action is pending.

(d) **Subpoena for Taking Deposition, Action Pending in Foreign Jurisdiction.** A subpoena for attendance at a deposition to be taken in Minnesota for an action pending in a foreign jurisdiction may be issued by the court administrator or by an attorney admitted to practice in Minnesota in the name of the court for the county in which the deposition will be taken, provided that the deposition is allowed and has been properly noticed under the law of the jurisdiction in which the action is pending. The subpoena may command the person to whom it is directed to produce and permit inspection and copying of designated books, papers, documents, electronically stored information, or tangible things that constitute or contain matters within the scope of the examination permitted by the law of the jurisdiction in which the action is pending, but in that event, the subpoena will be subject to the provisions of Rules 26.03 and 45.03(b)(2).

(e) **Notice to Parties.** Any use of a subpoena, other than to compel attendance at a trial, without prior notice to all parties to the action, is improper and may subject the party or attorney issuing it, or on whose behalf it was issued, to sanctions.

(Amended effective July 1, 2007.)

45.02. Service

(a) **Who May Serve and Method of Service; Timing of Notice.** A subpoena may be served by any person who is not a party and is not less than 18 years of age. Service of a subpoena upon a person named therein shall be made by delivering a copy thereof to such person or by leaving a copy at the person's usual place of abode with some person of suitable age and discretion then residing therein and, if the person's attendance is commanded, by tendering to that person the fees for one day's attendance and the mileage allowed by law. When the subpoena is issued on behalf of the state of Minnesota or an officer or agency thereof, fees and mileage need not be tendered. A subpoena commanding production for inspection, copying, testing, or sampling of designated books, papers, documents, or electronically stored information, tangible things, or inspection of premises, must be served on the subject of the subpoena, and notice of the required production must be served in the manner prescribed by Rule 5.02 on each party to the action, at least 7 days before the required production.

(b) **Statewide Service.** Subject to Rule 45.03(c)(1)(B), a subpoena may be served at any place within the state of Minnesota.

(c) **Proof of Service.** Proof of service when necessary shall be made by filing with the court administrator of the court on behalf of which the subpoena is issued a statement of the date and manner of service and of the names of the persons served, certified by the person who made the service.

(d) **Compensation of Subpoenaed Person.** The party serving the subpoena shall make arrangements for reasonable compensation as required under Rule 45.03(d) prior to the time of commanded production or the taking of such testimony. If such reasonable arrangements are not made, the person subpoenaed may proceed under Rule 45.03(c) or 45.03(b)(2). The party serving the subpoena may, if objection has been made, move upon notice to the deponent and all parties for an order directing the amount of such compensation at any time before the taking of the deposition. Any amounts paid shall be subject to the provisions of Rule 54.04.

(Amended effective July 1, 2010.)

45.03. Protection of Persons Subject to Subpoena

(a) **Requirement to Avoid Undue Burden.** A party or an attorney responsible for the issuance and service of a subpoena shall take reasonable steps to avoid imposing undue burden or expense on a person subject to that subpoena. The court on behalf of which the subpoena was issued shall enforce this duty and impose upon the party or attorney in breach of this duty an appropriate sanction, which may include, but is not limited to, lost earnings and a reasonable attorney's fee.

(b) **Subpoena for Document Production Without Deposition.**

(1) A person commanded to produce and permit inspection, copying, testing, or sampling of designated electronically stored information, books, papers, documents, or tangible things, or inspection of premises need not appear in person at the place of production or inspection unless commanded to appear for deposition, hearing, or trial.

(2) Subject to Rule 45.04(b), a person commanded to produce and permit inspection, copying, testing, or sampling may, within 14 days after service of the subpoena or before the time specified for compliance if such time is less than 14 days after service, serve upon the party or attorney designated in the subpoena written objection to producing any or all of the designated materials or inspection of the premises—or to producing electronically stored information in the form or forms requested. If objection is made, the party serving the subpoena shall not be entitled to inspect, copy, test, or sample the materials or inspect the premises except pursuant to an order of the court by which the subpoena was issued. If objection has been made, the party serving the subpoena may, upon notice to the person commanded

to produce, move at any time for an order to compel the production, inspection, copying, testing, or sampling. Such an order to compel production shall protect any person who is not a party or an officer of a party from significant expense resulting from the inspection, copying, testing, or sampling commanded.

(c) **Motion to Quash or Modify Subpoena.**

(1) On timely motion, the court on behalf of which a subpoena was issued shall quash or modify the subpoena if it
    (A) fails to allow reasonable time for compliance;
    (B) requires a person who is not a party or an officer of a party to travel to a place outside the county where that person resides, is employed or regularly transacts business in person, except that, subject to the provisions of Rule 45.03(c)(2)(C), such a person may in order to attend trial be commanded to travel from any such place within the state of Minnesota, or
    (C) requires disclosure of privileged or other protected matter and no exception or waiver applies, or
    (D) subjects a person to undue burden.

(2) If a subpoena
    (A) requires disclosure of a trade secret or other confidential research, development, or commercial information, or
    (B) requires disclosure of an unretained expert's opinion or information not describing specific events or occurrences in dispute and resulting from the expert's study made not at the request of any party, or
    (C) requires a person who is not a party or an officer of a party to incur substantial expense to travel outside the county where that person resides, is employed or regularly transacts business in person to attend trial, the court may, to protect a person subject to or affected by the subpoena, quash or modify the subpoena or, if the party in whose behalf the subpoena is issued shows a substantial need for the testimony or material that cannot be otherwise met without undue hardship and assures that the person to whom the subpoena is addressed will be reasonably compensated, the court may order appearance or production only upon specified conditions.

(d) **Compensation of Certain Non-Party Witnesses.** Subject to the provisions of Rules 26.02 and 26.03, a witness who is not a party to the action or an employee of a party [except a person appointed pursuant to Rule 30.02(f)] and who is required to give testimony or produce documents relating to a profession, business, or trade, or relating to knowledge, information, or facts obtained as a result of activities in such profession, business, or trade, is entitled to reasonable compensation for the time and expense involved in preparing for and giving such testimony or producing such documents.

(Amended effective July 1, 2007.)

45.04. Duties in Responding to Subpoena

(a) **Form of Production; Participation of Other Parties; Rescheduling.**

(1) A person responding to a subpoena to produce documents shall produce them as they are kept in the usual course of business or shall organize and label them to correspond with the categories in the demand.

(2) If a subpoena does not specify the form or forms for producing electronically stored information, a person responding to a subpoena must produce the information in a form or forms in which the person ordinarily maintains it or in a form or forms that are reasonably usable.

(3) A person responding to a subpoena need not produce the same electronically stored information in more than one form.

(4) A person responding to a subpoena need not provide discovery of electronically stored information from sources that the person identifies as not reasonably accessible because of undue burden or cost. On motion to compel discovery or to quash, the person from whom discovery is sought must show that the information sought is not reasonably accessible because of undue burden or cost. If that showing is made, the court may nonetheless order discovery from such sources if the requesting party shows good cause, considering the limitations of Rule 26.02(b)(3). The court may specify conditions for the discovery.

(5) The party issuing a subpoena for production or inspection shall make available to all parties any books, papers, documents or electronically stored information obtained from any person following issuance of a subpoena to that person. If production or inspection is made at a time or place, in a manner, or to an extent and scope, different from that commanded in the subpoena, the party issuing the subpoena must give notice to all parties to the action at least 7 days in advance of the rescheduled production. Any party may attend and participate in any noticed or rescheduled production or inspection and may also require production or inspection within the scope of the subpoena for inspection or copying.

(b) **Claims of Privilege.**

(1) When information subject to a subpoena is withheld on a claim that it is privileged or subject to protection as trial preparation materials, the claim shall be made expressly and shall be supported by a description of the nature of the documents, communications, or things not produced that is sufficient to enable the demanding party to contest the claim.

(2) If information is produced in response to a subpoena that is subject to a claim of privilege or of protection as trial-preparation material, the person making the claim may notify any party that received the information of the

claim and the basis for it. After being notified, a party must promptly return, sequester, or destroy the specified information and any copies it has and may not use or disclose the information until the claim is resolved. A receiving party may promptly present the information to the court under seal for a determination of the claim. If the receiving party disclosed the information before being notified, it must take reasonable steps to retrieve it. The person who produced the information must preserve the information until the claim is resolved.

(Amended effective July 1, 2010.)

45.05. Contempt

Failure by any person without adequate excuse to obey a subpoena served upon that person may be deemed a contempt of the court on behalf of which the subpoena was issued. An adequate cause for failure to obey exists when a subpoena purports to require a non-party to attend or produce at a place not within the limits provided by Rule 45.03(c)(1)(B).

Rule 45.06. Interstate Depositions and Discovery

(a) **Definitions.** In Rule 45.06:

    (1) "Foreign jurisdiction" means a state other than this state.

    (2) "Foreign subpoena" means a subpoena issued under authority of a court of record of a foreign jurisdiction.

    (3) "Person" means an individual, corporation, business trust, estate, trust, partnership, limited liability company, association, joint venture, public corporation, government, or governmental subdivision, agency or instrumentality, or any other legal or commercial entity.

    (4) "State" means a state of the United States, the District of Columbia, Puerto Rico, the United States Virgin Islands, or any territory or insular possession subject to the jurisdiction of the United States.

    (5) "Subpoena" means a document, however denominated, issued under authority of a court of record requiring a person to:

        (A) attend and give testimony at a deposition;

        (B) produce and permit inspection and copying of designated books, documents, records, electronically stored information, or tangible things in the possession, custody, or control of the person; or

        (C) permit inspection of premises under the control of the person.

(b) **Issuance of Subpoena.**

    (1) To request issuance of a subpoena under this section, a party must submit a foreign subpoena to the district court administrator of the court in the county in which discovery is sought to be conducted in this state. A request for the issuance of a subpoena under this act does not constitute an appearance in a

proceeding pursuant to Rule 5.01 of these rules, but does subject the filer to the jurisdiction of the court and to Minnesota law and rules, including the Minnesota Rules of Professional Conduct.

    (2)   A district court administrator in this state, upon submission of a foreign subpoena, shall, in accordance with that court's procedure, promptly issue a subpoena for service upon the person to which the foreign subpoena is directed.

    (3)   A subpoena under subsection (2) must:
        (A)   incorporate the terms used in the foreign subpoena; and
        (B)   contain or be accompanied by the names, addresses, and telephone numbers of all counsel of record in the proceeding to which the subpoena relates and of any party not represented by counsel.

(c)   **Service of Subpoena.** A subpoena issued by a district court administrator under Section (b) must be served in compliance with Rule 45.02 of these rules.

(d)   **Deposition, Production, and Inspection.** All Minnesota rules and statutes applicable to compliance with subpoenas to attend and give testimony, produce designated books, documents, records, electronically stored information, or tangible things, or permit inspection of premises apply to subpoenas issued under Paragraph (b).

(e)   **Application To Court.** An application to the court for a protective order or to enforce, quash, or modify a subpoena issued by a district court administrator under Paragraph (b) must comply with the rules and statutes of this state and be submitted to the district court in the county in which discovery is to be conducted.

(Adopted effective July 1, 2015.)

Advisory Committee Comment—2006 Amendment

Rule 45 is replaced, virtually in its entirety, by its federal counterpart. Provisions of the federal rule that do not apply in state court practice are deleted or replaced by comparable provisions consistent with current Minnesota practice. The new rule recognizes the scope of the subpoena power in the existing rule and does not significantly change it. Portions of the federal rule not relevant to state practice have been deleted. The rule adopts the language of the federal rules referring to the court where an action is pending. Because Minnesota allows actions to be commenced by service, the action is "pending" before the court named in the caption after service even though it is not on file with the court. See Minn. R. Civ. P. 3.01. The rule is not intended to change the existing practice that permitted subpoenas to be issued even though an action had not been filed.

The most significant "new" provisions of the rule are the authorization of issuance of subpoenas by attorneys as officers of the court (Rule 45.01(c)) and the adoption of a mechanism for requiring production of documents without requiring a deposition to be conducted (Rule 45.01(a)(3)). The rule retains the provisions of former Rule 45.06, which provide for expenses of non-parties put to particular expense of complying with a subpoena. Those provisions are now bifurcated, with portions relating to notice of the right to costs in Rule 45.01, dealing with the form of subpoenas, and the provision requiring payment in Rule 45.03(d). Additionally, Rule 45.03(a) places an affirmative duty on the attorney issuing or serving a subpoena to avoid imposing undue burden or expense on the person receiving it.

Advisory Committee Comment—2007 Amendment

Rule 45.01 is amended to add a process, in Rule 45.01(d), for issuance of a subpoena to compel attendance in Minnesota at a deposition in an action pending in another jurisdiction. The procedure in this section essentially follows that contained in former Rule 45.04(a), which was abrogated in 2005.

Rule 45.01(e) is a new rule intended to clarify the existing rule because of continuing confusion over the need to provide notice to all parties before issuance of a subpoena for pretrial discovery. Existing Rule 45.02(a) explicitly requires notice, but that provision has been overlooked in a number of instances reported to the advisory committee. Accordingly, Rule 45.01(e) is included to make the requirement of notice more prominent and to make it clearly apply to every use of a subpoena prior to trial. The rule does not specify the form of notice required, but it would normally be accomplished by providing either a copy of the subpoena at the time it is served on the non-party or by unambiguous notice in some other way that a non-party is being subpoenaed.

Rule 45.02(d) is amended to establish an explicit deadline for making arrangements for compensation by a party receiving a subpoena that requires only the production of documents without a deposition. By adding the words "commanded production or" to the first sentence, the rule applies explicitly to this situation, and establishes the same deadline as for a deposition.

Rule 45 is also amended to include provisions for use of subpoenas to obtain discovery of electronically stored information. These amendments relate to the discovery of electronically stored information, and generally just incorporate into Rule 45 for subpoena practice the procedures of Rules 26, 30, 33, 34, and 37 for discovery from parties.

Advisory Committee Comment—2010 Amendment

Rule 45 is amended in several ways to prevent misuse of subpoenas. These amendments are consistent with the purpose of two provisions of the existing rule. Under Rule 45.01(e), notice of issuance of a subpoena is required in order that all parties have an opportunity to participate in the production and to curtail use of a subpoena for ex parte investigation. Rule 45.03(a) explicitly recognizes that the costs of discovery from non-parties should be borne, to the extent feasible, by the parties to the action and the burden on subpoenaed parties should be minimized. The amendment in 2010 adds language to Rule 45.02(a) that is intended to make even more explicit the proper notice for use of a subpoena for production of documents, etc.

Rule 45.04(a) is amended by the addition of paragraph (5) that is intended to reinforce that the proper use of a subpoena for production is to obtain information for use by all parties to the litigation, and not for ex parte use by a single party. Once a subpoena is issued to a non-party, information produced or testimony by that non-party must be made available to all parties. The new language also facilitates the orderly production of information. Rule 45 was amended in 2006 to permit use of subpoenas to require production of documents and other information from non-parties without requiring a deposition to be scheduled and, indeed, without even requiring a personal appearance. See Rule 45.03(b). Where the non-party and the party that issued a subpoena make alternative arrangements for production in response to the subpoena—which may be entirely proper—

the potential exists that the production would occur without the knowledge of the other parties to the action. That production, without notice to the parties, is improper and essentially prevents participation by the parties who had received notice of another time of production. The amended rule places a duty on the party issuing the subpoena either to arrange production at a time agreeable to all parties and the non-party or to give notice to the other parties.

The amended rule is intended to create a streamlined process that minimizes the burdens of discovery on non-parties and reinforces the rights of all parties to participate in court-sanctioned discovery on an equal footing. There may still be circumstances where other parties will want to serve separate subpoenas to the same non-party, either to request additional documents or inspection or copying, or to obtain documents in a different format. Ideally, the parties will coordinate their efforts to minimize the costs and other burdens of production on the person receiving a subpoena.

Notice of the intention to comply with a subpoena in some manner other than that noticed in the subpoena is important because one of the parties may have valid objections to the production taking place at all. Under the revised rule, no production can properly occur without all parties having at least seven days' notice, providing any party the opportunity either to participate in the production or to seek a protective order to prevent the production from taking place. Because of the expedited hearing requirement for commitment proceedings under Minn. Stat. ch. 253B, subpoenas for production in those proceedings are subject to a 24-hour notice requirement as provided in a new Rule 25 added to the Special Rules of Procedure Governing Proceedings Under the Minnesota Commitment and Treatment Act.

Advisory Committee Comments—2015 Amendments

Rule 45.06 is a new rule, recommended to adopt the Uniform Interstate Deposition and Discovery Act, promulgated by the National Conference of Commissioners on Uniform State Laws in 2007.

This rule allows issuance of a subpoena in Minnesota based upon the proper issuance and service of a subpoena under the authority of another state. If a Minnesota subpoena is issued, the procedures of Rule 45 apply to the service and enforcement of that subpoena and other procedures relating to it. Notice must be provided to all other parties to the action, and the form of subpoena must conform to Minnesota law. Minnesota citizens and residents are entitled to the full protection of Minnesota's rules even where the subpoena is initiated for use in foreign proceedings.

Although adopted as a rule, rather than a statute, recognizing the Minnesota Supreme Court's inherent and exclusive authority over matters of court procedure, the rule retains the operative provisions of the Uniform Act. Like uniform laws, this rule should be interpreted to accomplish uniformity among the states and should be construed to promote that purpose. See Minn. Stat. § 645.22. Construction of the uniform law by other states may accordingly be relevant to its interpretation in Minnesota. See generally Layne-Minn. Co. v. Regents of the Univ. of Minn., 266 Minn. 284, 123 N.W.2d 371 (1963).

RULE 46. EXCEPTIONS UNNECESSARY

Formal exceptions to rulings or orders of the court are unnecessary; but for all purposes for which an exception has heretofore been taken it is sufficient that a party, at the time the ruling or order of the court is made or sought, makes known to the court the action which the party desires the court to take or any objection to the action of the court and the grounds therefor; and, if a party has no opportunity to object to a ruling or order at the time it is made, the absence of an objection does not thereafter prejudice the party. A minute of the objection to the ruling or order shall be made by the judge or reporter.

RULE 47. JURORS

Rule 47.01. Examination of Jurors

The court may permit the parties or their attorneys to conduct the examination of prospective jurors or may itself conduct the examination. In the latter event, the court shall permit the parties or their attorneys to supplement the examination by such further inquiry as it deems proper. Supplemental juror questionnaires completed by jurors shall not be accessible to the public unless formally admitted into evidence in a publicly accessible hearing or trial

(Amended effective July 1, 2005.)

Advisory Committee Comment - 2005 Amendments

The addition of the last sentence in Rule 47.01 precluding public access to completed supplemental juror questionnaires recognizes both the legitimate privacy interests of jurors and the interests of the public in otherwise publicly accessible court proceedings. This rule does not apply to juror qualification questionnaires submitted by jurors in accordance with Minn. Gen. R. Prac. 807; public access to completed qualification questionnaires is governed by Minn. Gen. R. Prac. 814.

Rule 47.02

(Abrogated effective January 1, 1999.)

Rule 47.03. Separation of Jury

After the jury has retired for its deliberations, the court, in its discretion, may permit the jury to separate overnight and return to its deliberations the following morning.

Rule 47.04. Excuse

The court may for good cause excuse a juror from service during trial or deliberation.

(Added effective January 1, 1999.)

Advisory Committee Comment - 1998 Amendments

Rule 47.02 is abrogated. Under this amendment, alternate jurors are no longer part of the jury trial process. Rather than seat "alternate" jurors who will, or may, then participate in the deliberations, the rule simply does not provide for two classes of jurors. Jurors who begin the case by being sworn in as jurors continue to the discharge of the jury, unless they are excused for cause as provided for by Rule 47.04. This amendment parallels the abandonment of using alternates in federal court in 1991, and is intended to resolve an ongoing source of dissatisfaction with jury service by jurors. See Fed.R.Civ.P. 47(b), Notes of Advisory Comm. - 1991 Amends., reprinted in Federal Civil Judicial Procedure and Rules 205 (West 1998).

Rule 47.04 is new and is identical to Fed.R.Civ.P. 47(c). Although courts presently have the inherent power to excuse jurors even in the absence of a rule, there is no reason to have the federal rule be different from the state rule on this issue. Other than obviating confusion over whether there might be some substantive difference in intent, this amendment is not intended to change the existing practice. See Minnesota Statutes, section 546.13 (1996) (codifying authority to excuse juror).

RULE 48. NUMBER OF JURORS; PARTICIPATION IN VERDICT

The court shall seat a jury of not fewer than six and not more than twelve members and all jurors shall participate in the verdict unless excused from service by the court pursuant to Rule 47.04. Unless otherwise provided by law or the parties otherwise stipulate, (1) the verdict shall be unanimous and (2) no verdict shall be taken from a jury reduced in size to fewer than six members.

(Amended effective January 1, 1999.)

Advisory Committee Comment - 1998 Amendments

This rule requires the court to permit all jurors to participate in deliberations. Rule 47.02 is abrogated to abolish alternate jurors, and Rule 48 expressly provides that all jurors participate in the deliberations. The rule prohibits a verdict from a jury of fewer than six jurors, unless the parties agree to a lesser number.

The rule does not provide any constraints on what size jury is appropriate in any particular case. Practical considerations of cost, courtroom design, and imposition on potential jurors as well as those seated may militate toward a jury of six. Where the trial is likely to be long, or where other considerations make it likely that jurors will need to be excused from service, more than six jurors should be seated. The rule also permits a twelve-person jury as was historically used in civil trials. Juries of twelve significantly reduce the likelihood of unusual or aberrant jury verdicts, and should be considered where the issues are unusually complex or important, or present difficult fact-finding challenges to the jury. See generally Developments in the Law - The Civil Jury, 110 Harv.L.Rev. 1408, 1468-80 (1997).

This rule expressly mandates seating a jury of from six to twelve jurors. Seating a larger jury is not provided for, and should be considered only in very unusual circumstances where more than six jurors are likely to be excused, making it inevitable that fewer than six will remain. Rather than risk a mistrial in that situation, the court should seek a stipulation of the parties that a verdict may be taken from a jury smaller than six. See generally Manual for Complex Litigation section 22.41 and n.408 (3rd ed. 1995). It may be permissible to seat a jury of larger than twelve, so long as twelve or fewer remain for deliberations, but there is no clear authority or precedent for this. If the parties stipulate to a larger jury, it should certainly not be error to seat one. The last sentence of the rule requires a verdict to be unanimous unless there is an agreement to a less-than-unanimous verdict or it is otherwise provided by law. Both the Minnesota Constitution and statutory law allow verdicts in civil cases, even without stipulation of the parties, to be returned by 5/6ths of the jurors after six hours of deliberations. See Minn. Const. art. I, section 4 and Minnesota Statutes section 546.17 (1996). Where jury of more than six, but fewer than twelve, jurors deliberates, a 6/7ths, 7/8ths, 8/9ths, 9/10ths or 10/11ths verdict is permitted. For a twelve-person jury, ten of the twelve jurors (the equivalent of 5/6ths) can return a verdict.

RULE 49. SPECIAL VERDICTS AND INTERROGATORIES

49.01. Special Verdicts

(a) The court may require a jury to return only a special verdict in the form of a special written finding upon each issue of fact. In that event the court may submit to the jury written questions susceptible of categorical or other brief answer or may submit written forms of the several special findings which might properly be made under the pleadings and evidence; or it may use such other method of submitting the issues and require written findings thereon as it deems most appropriate. The court shall give to the jury such explanations and instructions concerning the matter thus submitted as may be necessary to enable the jury to make its findings upon each issue. If in so doing the court omits any issue of fact raised by the pleadings or by the evidence, each party waives the right to a trial by jury of the issue so omitted unless before the jury retires the party demands its submission to the jury. As to an issue omitted without such demand, the court may make a finding; or, if it fails to do so, it shall be deemed to have made a finding in accord with the judgment on the special verdict. Except as provided in Rule 49.01(b), neither the court nor counsel shall inform the jury of the effect of its answers on the outcome of the case.

(b) In actions involving Minnesota Statutes, chapter 604 the court shall inform the jury of the effect of its answers to the comparative fault question and shall permit counsel to comment thereon, unless the court is of the opinion that doubtful or unresolved questions of law or complex issues of law or fact are involved which may render such instruction or comment erroneous, misleading, or confusing to the jury.

49.02. General Verdict Accompanied by Answer to Interrogatories

The court may submit to the jury, together with appropriate forms for a general verdict, written interrogatories upon one or more issues of fact the decision of which is necessary to a verdict. The court shall give such explanation or instruction as may be necessary to enable the jury both to make answers to the interrogatories and to render a general verdict, and the court shall direct the jury both to make written answers and to render a general verdict. When the general verdict and the answers are harmonious, the court shall direct the entry of the appropriate judgment upon the verdict and answers. When the answers are consistent with each other, but one or more is inconsistent with the general verdict, the court may direct the entry of judgment in accordance with the answers, notwithstanding the general verdict, or may return the jury for further consideration of its answers and verdict, or may order a new trial. When the answers are inconsistent with each other and one or more is likewise inconsistent with the general verdict, the court shall not direct the entry of judgment, but may return the jury for further consideration of its answers and verdict, or may order a new trial.

RULE 50. JUDGMENT AS A MATTER OF LAW IN JURY TRIALS; ALTERNATIVE MOTION FOR NEW TRIAL; CONDITIONAL RULINGS

50.01. Judgment as a Matter of Law During Trial

(a) **Standard.** If during a trial by jury a party has been fully heard on an issue and there is no legally sufficient evidentiary basis for a reasonable jury to find for that party on that issue, the court may decide the issue against that party and may grant a motion for judgment as a matter of law against that party with respect to a claim or defense that cannot under the controlling law be maintained or defeated without a favorable finding on that issue.

(b) **Timing and Content.** Motions for judgment as a matter of law during trial may be made at any time before submission of the case to the jury. Such a motion shall specify the judgment sought and the law and the facts on which the moving party is entitled to the judgment.

50.02. Making or Renewing Motion for Judgment After Trial; Alternative Motion for New Trial

If, for any reason, the court does not grant a motion for judgment as a matter of law made during trial, the court is considered to have submitted the action to the jury subject to the court's later deciding the legal questions raised by the motion. Whether or not the party has moved for judgment as a matter of law before submission of the case to the jury, a party may make or renew a request for judgment as a matter of law by serving a motion within the time specified in Rule 59 for the service of a motion for a new trial—and may alternatively request a new trial or join a motion for new trial under Rule 59. In ruling on such a motion, the court may:

(a) if a verdict was returned:
 (1) allow the judgment to stand,
 (2) order a new trial, or
 (3) direct entry of judgment as a matter of law; or

(b) if no verdict was returned:
 (1) order a new trial, or
 (2) direct entry of judgment as a matter of law.

50.03. Granting Motion for Judgment as a Matter of Law; Conditional Rulings; New Trial Motion

(a) **Conditional Rulings.** If the motion for judgment as a matter of law is granted, the court shall also rule on the motion for a new trial, if any, by determining whether it should be granted if the judgment is thereafter vacated or reversed, and shall specify the grounds for granting or denying the motion for the new trial. If the motion for a new trial is thus conditionally granted, the order thereon does not affect the finality of the judgment. In case the motion for a new trial has been conditionally granted and the judgment is reversed on appeal, the new trial shall proceed unless the appellate court has otherwise ordered. In case the motion for a new trial has been conditionally denied, the respondent on appeal may assert error in that denial; and if the judgment is reversed on appeal, subsequent proceedings shall be in accordance with the order of the appellate court.

(b) **Timing.** Any motion for a new trial under Rule 59 by a party against whom judgment as a matter of law is rendered shall be served and heard within the times specified in Rule 59 for the service and hearing of a motion for a new trial.

50.04. Denial of Motion for Judgment as a Matter of Law

If the motion for judgment as a matter of law is denied, the party who prevailed on that motion may, as respondent on appeal, assert grounds entitling the party to a new trial in the event the appellate court concludes that the trial court erred in denying the motion for judgment. If the appellate court reverses the judgment, nothing in this rule precludes it from determining that the respondent is entitled to a new trial, or from directing the trial court to determine whether a new trial shall be granted.

(Amended January 9, 2006, effective January 2, 2006.)

Advisory Committee Comment--2000 Amendments

Although the text of this Rule 50.02 is not changed substantively by these amendments, it is worth noting that Rule 59.03, governing the time for the time from 15 days to 30 days for filing the motion and from 30 days to 60 days for having the motion heard. This amendment as the practical effect of extending the time for filing a motion under Rule 50 because Rule 50.02(c) incorporates the filing and hearing time limits of Rule 59.

Advisory Committee Comment—2006 Amendment

Rule 50 is amended in toto to adopt various changes made in 1991 to Fed. R. Civ. P. 50. The 1991 amendment of the federal rule was made to remove the archaic language and procedures of directing verdicts and granting j.n.o.v. The amended rule states a standard that the former rule already recognized: a uniform standard for motions made after trial begins of a "motion for judgment as a matter of law." The purpose of the change is two-fold: to adopt names that better describe the role of the motions and, because the motions essentially apply the same standard, to give them a common name.

This change is not intended to change substantive practice relating to these motions. The federal rule amendment in 1991 was not intended to change the actual practice under that rule. See Fed. R. Civ. P. 50(a), Advisory Comm. Notes—1991 Amend. The federal courts have recognized the non-substantive nature of the amendment. See 9A CHARLES ALAN WRIGHT & ARTHUR R. MILLER, FEDERAL PRACTICE & PROCEDURE § 2521, at 243 n.15 and accompanying text (2d ed. 1995) (collecting cases).

Minnesota practice differs from federal practice in one important respect—former Fed. R. Civ. P. 50 did not have the express provision of Minn. R. Civ. P. 50.02(a) allowing a motion for judgment n.o.v. to be brought "whether or not the party has moved for a directed verdict," and the current version of Fed. R. Civ. P. 50 lacks equivalent language with regard to motions for judgment as a matter of law. Because the amended Minnesota Rule 50.02 is not intended to change Minnesota practice in this respect, the amended rule retains the concept that a motion for judgment as a matter of law may be brought after submission of the case to the jury, whether or not such a motion was brought before submission to the jury.

The timing provisions of the federal rule have been changed slightly to accommodate Minnesota procedure including that relating to the service and filing of post-decision motions. Like the current rule, motions under Rule 50 must be served and filed in accordance with the timing mechanism and deadlines of Minn. R. Civ. P. 59.

RULE 51. INSTRUCTIONS TO THE JURY; OBJECTIONS; PRESERVING A CLAIM OF ERROR

51.01. Requests

(a) **At or Before the Close of Evidence.** A party may, at the close of the evidence or at an earlier reasonable time that the court directs, file and furnish to every other party written requests that the court instruct the jury on the law as set forth in the requests.

(b) **After the Close of Evidence.** After the close of the evidence, a party may:
(1) file requests for instructions on issues that could not reasonably have been anticipated at an earlier time for requests set under Rule 51.01(a), and
(2) with the court's permission file untimely requests for instructions on any issue.

51.02. Instructions

The court:

(a) must inform the parties of its proposed instructions and proposed action on the requests before instructing the jury and before final jury arguments;

(b) must give the parties an opportunity to object on the record and out of the jury's hearing to the proposed instructions and actions on requests before the instructions and arguments are delivered; and

(c) may instruct the jury at any time after trial begins and before the jury is discharged.

51.03. Objections

(a) **Form.** A party who objects to an instruction or the failure to give an instruction must do so on the record, stating distinctly the matter objected to and the grounds of the objection.

(b) **Timeliness.** An objection is timely if:
  (1) a party that has been informed of an instruction or action on a request before the jury is instructed and before final jury arguments, as provided by Rule 51.02(a), objects at the opportunity for objection required by Rule 51.02(b); or
  (2) a party that has not been informed of an instruction or action on a request before the time for objection provided under Rule 51.02(b) objects promptly after learning that the instruction or request will be, or has been, given or refused.

51.04. Assigning Error; Plain Error

(a) **Assigned Error.** A party may assign as error:
  (1) an error in an instruction actually given if that party made a proper objection under Rule 51.03, or
  (2) a failure to give an instruction if that party made a proper request under Rule 51.01, and—unless the court made a definitive ruling on the record rejecting the request—also made a proper objection under Rule 51.03.

(b) **Plain Error.** A court may consider a plain error in the instructions affecting substantial rights that has not been preserved as required by Rule 51.04(a)(1) or (2).

(Amended effective January 1, 2006.)

Advisory Committee Comment - 1998 Amendments

The Committee does not believe a mandatory rule requiring use of written instructions in all cases is appropriate, but notes the widespread use of written instructions and the near-unanimous support for written instructions among judges, lawyers, and commentators. See, e.g., American Bar Association, Section of Litigation, Civil Trial Practice Standards, section 5(f), at 16 (1998) ("Final instructions should be provided for the jurors' use during deliberation."). If written instructions are given, the Committee believes that the court should have the discretion to decide that more than one complete copy of the instructions be taken to the jury room when the jury retires to deliberate.

Advisory Committee Comment—2006 Amendment

Rule 51 is entirely new with this amendment. The new rule is modeled on its federal counterpart, Fed. R. Civ. P. 51, as it was amended in 2003. The changes are intended primarily to provide detailed procedural guidance where the existing rule is either silent or vague. See generally Fed. R. Civ. P. 51, Advis. Comm. Notes—2003 Amend., reprinted in FED. CIV. JUD. PROC. & RULES 227 (West 2005 ed.).

Rule 51.02(c) continues to recognize that the court may give instructions to the jury at any time after trial begins, including preliminary instructions before opening statements or the taking of evidence, during the trial, and at the end of trial either before or after the arguments of counsel.

RULE 52. FINDINGS BY THE COURT

52.01. Effect

In all actions tried upon the facts without a jury or with an advisory jury, the court shall find the facts specially and state separately its conclusions of law thereon and direct the entry of the appropriate judgment; and in granting or refusing interlocutory injunctions the court shall similarly set forth the findings of fact and conclusions of law which constitute the grounds for its action. Requests for findings are not necessary for purposes of review. Findings of fact, whether based on oral or documentary evidence, shall not be set aside unless clearly erroneous, and due regard shall be given to the opportunity of the trial court to judge the credibility of the witnesses. The findings of a referee, to the extent adopted by the court, shall be considered as the findings of the court. It will be sufficient if the findings of fact and conclusions of law are stated orally and recorded in open court following the close of the evidence or appear in an opinion or memorandum of decision filed by the court or in an accompanying memorandum. Findings of fact and conclusions of law are unnecessary on decisions on motions pursuant to Rule 12 or 56 or any other motion except as provided in Rules 23.08(c) and 41.02.

Advisory Committee Comment—2006 Amendment

Rule 52.01 is amended to renumber one of the rule cross-references to reflect the amendment and renumbering of Rule 23 as part of the amendments effective January 1, 2006.

52.02. Amendment

Upon motion of a party served and heard not later than the time allowed for a motion for new trial pursuant to Rule 59.03, the court may amend its findings or make additional findings, and may amend the judgment accordingly if judgment has been entered. The motion may be made with a motion for a new trial and may be made on the files, exhibits, and minutes of the court. When findings of fact are made in actions tried by the court without a jury, the question of the sufficiency of the evidence to support the findings may thereafter be raised whether or not the party raising the question has made in the district court an objection to such findings or has made a motion to amend them or a motion for judgment.

(Amended effective March 1, 2001.)

Advisory Committee Comment--2000 Amendments

Although the text of this Rule 52.02 is not changed substantively by these amendments, it is worth noting that Rule 59.03, governing the time for filing a motion for a new trial is changed to expand the time from 15 days to 30 days for filing motion and from 30 days to 60 days for having the motion heard. This amendment has the practical effect of extending the time for filing a motion for amended findings under Rule 52 because Rule 52.02 incorporates the filing and hearing time limits of Rule 59.

RULE 53. MASTERS

53.01. Appointment

(a) **Authority for Appointment.** Unless a statute provides otherwise, a court may appoint a master only to:
   (1) perform duties consented to by the parties;
   (2) hold trial proceedings and make or recommend findings of fact on issues to be decided by the court without a jury if appointment is warranted by
      (A) some exceptional condition, or
      (B) the need to perform an accounting or resolve a difficult computation of damages; or
   (3) address pretrial and post-trial matters that cannot be addressed effectively and timely by an available district judge.

(b) **Disqualification.** A master must not have a relationship to the parties, counsel, action, or court that would require disqualification of a judge, unless the parties consent with the court's approval to appointment of a particular person after disclosure of any potential grounds for disqualification.

(c) **Expense.** In appointing a master, the court must consider the fairness of imposing the likely expenses on the parties and must protect against unreasonable expense or delay.

53.02. Order Appointing Master

(a) **Notice.** The court must give the parties notice and an opportunity to be heard before appointing a master. A party may suggest candidates for appointment.

(b) **Contents.** The order appointing a master must direct the master to proceed with all reasonable diligence and must state:
   (1) the master's duties, including any investigation or enforcement duties, and any limits on the master's authority under Rule 53.03;
   (2) the circumstances—if any—in which the master may communicate ex parte with the court or a party;
   (3) the nature of the materials to be preserved and filed as the record of the master's activities;
   (4) the time limits, method of filing the record, other procedures, and standards for reviewing the master's orders, findings, and recommendations;
   (5) the basis, terms, and procedure for fixing the master's compensation under Rule 53.08; and
   (6) the extent to which, if at all, the parties and the master must use the court's E-Filing System in the proceedings before the master.

(c) **Entry of Order.** The court may enter the order appointing a master only after the master has filed an affidavit disclosing whether there is any ground for disqualification and, if a ground for disqualification is disclosed, after the parties have consented with the court's approval to waive the disqualification.

(d) **Amendment.** The order appointing a master may be amended at any time after notice to the parties and an opportunity to be heard.

(Amended effective July 1, 2015.)

Advisory Committee Comments—2015 Amendments

Rule 53.02(b) is amended to add a new subdivision (6) that expressly requires the court's appointment order to address the extent to which the parties and an appointed master must use the court's E-Filing System. This provision recognizes that a particular master may not otherwise be a registered user of the court's E-Filing System, and it may be appropriate either to direct that the parties and the master use the system for all service and filing or in the rare case, to excuse the master and parties from doing so.

53.03. Master's Authority

Unless the appointing order expressly directs otherwise, a master has authority to regulate all proceedings and take all appropriate measures to perform fairly and efficiently the assigned duties. The master may by order impose upon a party any noncontempt sanction provided by Rule 37 or 45, and may recommend a contempt sanction against a party and sanctions against a nonparty.

53.04. Evidentiary Hearings

Unless the appointing order expressly directs otherwise, a master conducting an evidentiary hearing may exercise the power of the appointing court to compel, take, and record evidence.

53.05. Master's Orders

A master who makes an order must file the order and promptly serve a copy on each party. The court administrator must enter the order on the docket.

53.06. Master's Reports

A master must report to the court as required by the order of appointment. The master must file the report and promptly serve a copy of the report on each party unless the court directs otherwise.

53.07. Action on Master's Order, Report, or Recommendations

(a) **Action.** In acting on a master's order, report, or recommendations, the court must afford an opportunity to be heard and may receive evidence, and may: adopt or affirm; modify; wholly or partly reject or reverse; or resubmit to the master with instructions.

(b) **Time To Object or Move.** A party may file objections to—or a motion to adopt or modify—the master's order, report, or recommendations no later than 21 days from the time the master's order, report, or recommendations are served, unless the court sets a different time.

(c) **Fact Findings.** The court must decide de novo all objections to findings of fact made or recommended by a master unless the parties stipulate with the court's consent that:
(1) the master's findings will be reviewed for clear error, or
(2) the findings of a master appointed under Rule 53.01(a)(1) or
(3) will be final.

(d) **Legal Conclusions.** The court must decide de novo all objections to conclusions of law made or recommended by a master.

(e) **Procedural Matters.** Unless the order of appointment establishes a different standard of review, the court may set aside a master's ruling on a procedural matter only for an abuse of discretion.

(Amended effective January 1, 2020.)

53.08. Compensation

(a) **Fixing Compensation.** The court must fix the master's compensation before or after judgment on the basis and terms stated in the order of appointment, but the court may set a new basis and terms after notice and an opportunity to be heard.

(b) **Payment.** The compensation fixed under Rule 53.08(a) must be paid either:
(1) by a party or parties; or
(2) from a fund or subject matter of the action within the court's control.

(c) **Allocation.** The court must allocate payment of the master's compensation among the parties after considering the nature and amount of the controversy, the means of the parties, and the extent to which any party is more responsible than other parties for the reference to a master. An interim allocation may be amended to reflect a decision on the merits.

53.09. Appointment of Statutory Referee

A statutory referee employed in the judicial branch is subject to this rule only when the order referring a matter to the statutory referee expressly provides that the reference is made under this rule.

Advisory Committee Comment—2006 Amendment

Rule 53 is replaced by a new rule derived nearly verbatim from its federal counterpart, Fed. R. Civ. P. 53. The federal rule was extensively revised by amendment in 2003. That amendment was taken up by the federal advisory committee after it had received empirical research on the use of masters in federal court. See THOMAS E. WILLGING ET AL., SPECIAL MASTERS' INCIDENCE AND ACTIVITY (Fed. Jud. Ctr. 2000).

The federal rule provides significantly more detailed guidance to courts and litigants on the proper use of masters than either its predecessor or the current Minnesota rule. The committee believes that the changes to the federal rule are thoughtful and are valuable to litigants, and therefore appropriate for adoption in Minnesota.

The rule is not intended to expand the use of masters, but is designed to make the use of masters more readily accomplished in the minority of cases where their use is warranted.

Rule 53.01 includes specific guidance on the circumstances justifying or permitting the appointment of a master. Most significantly, the rule clarifies that in the absence of consent a master cannot be assigned to try issues on which the parties are entitled to a jury trial; mere press of other business would not trump the jury trial right. Although the court has greater latitude under the rule for issues triable to the court, either consent or some truly exceptional circumstances must be present. Short of trying issues, however, there are many roles that masters may play in civil cases, particularly in complex cases where the parties consent to the appointment. See generally Lynn Jokela & David F. Herr, Special Masters in State Court Complex Litigation: An Available and Underused Case Management Tool, 31 WM. MITCHELL L. REV. 1299 (2005).

Rule 53.02 establishes specific requirements for the order appointing a master. These subjects reflect a form of "best practices" for the use of masters, and they define procedures to be followed upon referral to a master. The rule intentionally makes these provisions mandatory because they are matters prone to dispute if not resolved at the time of appointment.

Rule 53.03 clarifies the extent of a master's authority and defines those powers expansively within the confines of the duties assigned to the master. The rule explicitly authorizes the imposition of discovery sanctions other than contempt by a master, and allows a master to recommend imposition of contempt sanctions.

The procedures established under Rule 53.07 are intended to clarify the role of master and ensure that all parties, including the appointing judge and appointed master, understand the master's role. The standards of review of a master's decisions are particularly important to the parties and the court, and are set forth with special detail.

Compensation of masters under this rule should be established in the order of appointment. See Rule 53.02(b)(5). In the majority of cases, compensation will be ordered to be paid by the parties pursuant to Rule 53.08(b)(1). The provision of Rule 53.08(b)(2) provides for payment from a fund created by the litigation, as where fees are awarded under the "common fund" doctrine, or by a fund that is the subject matter of the litigation. The federal rule advisory committee has recognized that it may be appropriate to revise the allocation ordered on an interim basis once the action is concluded. See Fed. R. Civ. P. 53(h), Advis. Comm. Notes—2003 Amend., reprinted in FED. CIV. JUD. PROC. & RULES 237 (West 2005 ed.).

Rule 53.09 distinguishes between masters under this rule, and regular court employees authorized as "referees" by statute. "Statutory referees" as used in the rule refers to court employees, whether full- or part-time, who serve regularly in multiple cases or calendars. See, e.g., Minn. Stat. §§ 260.031 (juvenile court referees authorized); 484.013, subd. 3 (referees authorized for housing calendar consolidation program);

484.70 (referees generally in district court); 491A.03, subd. 1 (2004) (referees in conciliation court in second and fourth districts). In certain situations, a "referee" appointed pursuant to statute for a single case should be viewed as a master under Rule 53. See, e.g., Minn. Stat. §§ 116B.05 (referee in particular environmental action); 558.04 (2004) (referees for partition of real estate). The procedures governing statutory referees are generally found in the statutes authorizing their use.

Advisory Committee Comment—2020 Amendments

Rule 53.07(b) is amended as part of the extensive amendments made to the timing provisions of the rules. These amendments implement the adoption of a standard "day" for counting deadlines under the rules—counting all days regardless of the length of the period and standardizing the time periods, where practicable, to a 7-, 14-, 21- or 28-day schedule. The only change to this rule changes the 20-day period to file a response to a master's decision to 21 days. This change affects only the time limits, and is not intended to have any other effect.

RULE 54. JUDGMENTS; COSTS

54.01. Definition; Form

Judgment as used in these rules includes a decree and means the final determination of the rights of the parties in an action or proceeding. A judgment shall not contain a recital of pleadings, the report of a referee, or the record of prior proceedings.

54.02. Judgment upon Multiple Claims

When multiple claims for relief or multiple parties are involved in an action, the court may direct the entry of a final judgment as to one or more but fewer than all of the claims or parties only upon an express determination that there is no just reason for delay and upon an express direction for the entry of judgment. In the absence of such determination and direction, any order or other form of decision, however designated, which adjudicates fewer than all the claims or the rights and liabilities of fewer than all the parties shall not terminate the action as to any of the claims or parties, and the order or other form of decision is subject to revision at any time before the entry of judgment adjudicating all the claims and the rights and liabilities of all the parties.

54.03. Demand for Judgment

A judgment by default shall not be different in kind from or exceed in amount that prayed for in the demand for judgment. Except as to a party against whom a judgment is entered by default, every other judgment shall grant the relief to which the party in whose favor it is rendered is entitled.

54.04. Costs

(a) **Costs and disbursements allowed.** Costs and disbursements shall be allowed as provided by law.

(b) **Application for costs and disbursements.** A party seeking to recover costs and disbursements must serve and file a detailed sworn application for taxation of costs and disbursements with the court administrator, substantially in the form as published by the State Court Administrator. The application must be signed under oath or penalty of perjury pursuant to Minn. Stat. § 358.116, and must be served and filed not later than 45 days after entry of a final judgment as to the party seeking costs and disbursements. A party may, but is not required to, serve and file a memorandum of law with an application for taxation of costs and disbursements.

(c) **Objections.** Not later than 7 days after service of the application by any party, any other party may file a separate application as in section (b), above, or may file written objections to the award of any costs or disbursements sought by any other party, specifying the grounds for each objection.

(d) **Decision.** Costs and disbursements may be taxed by the court administrator or a district court judge at any time after all parties have been allowed an opportunity to file applications and to object to the application of any other party as provided in this rule. The judge or court administrator may tax any costs and disbursements allowed by law.

(e) **Review by Judge.** If costs and disbursements are taxed by the court administrator, any party aggrieved by the action of the court administrator may serve and file a notice of appeal not later than 7 days after the court administrator serves notice of taxation on all parties. Any other party may file a response to the appeal not later than 7 days after the appeal is served. The appeal shall thereupon be decided by a district court judge and determined upon the record before the court administrator.

(f) **Judgment for Costs.** When costs and disbursements have been determined, whether by a district court judge or by the court administrator with no appeal taken to a district court judge, they shall promptly be inserted in the judgment.

(Amended effective July 1, 2015.)

Advisory Committee Comment—2010 Amendment

Rule 54.04 is amended both to clarify its operation and to improve the procedure for taxing costs by the court administrator and the review of those decisions by the district court judge. The amended process is commenced by filing an application on a form established by the State Court Administrator and made available on the Judicial Branch website (or in substantially the same form).

Advisory Committee Comments—2015 Amendments

Rule 54.04 is amended to implement a new statute directing the courts to consider accepting documents without notarization if they are signed under the following language: "I declare under penalty of perjury that everything I have stated in this document is true and correct." Minn. Stat. § 358.116 (2014) (codifying 2014 Minn. Laws ch. 204, § 3). The statute allows the courts to require specifically by rule that notarization is necessary, but the difficulty in accomplishing and documenting notarization for documents that are e-filed and e-served militates against requiring formal notarization. Accordingly, cost applications may be signed by the party under penalty of perjury, so long as the appropriate language is included above the party's signature. The rule also requires inclusion of the date of signing and the county and state where signed to provide information necessary to establish the fact and venue of possible perjury; this information is otherwise provided by notarization. Rule 15 of the Minnesota General Rules of Practice provides that documents signed in accordance with its terms constitute "affidavits."

RULE 55. DEFAULT

55.01. Judgment

When a party against whom a judgment for affirmative relief is sought has failed to plead or otherwise defend within the time allowed therefor by these rules or by statute, and that fact is made to appear by affidavit, judgment by default shall be entered against that party as follows:

(a) When the plaintiff's claim against a defendant is upon a contract for the payment of money only, or for the payment of taxes and penalties and interest thereon owing to the state, the court administrator, upon request of the plaintiff and upon affidavit of the amount due, which may not exceed the amount demanded in the complaint or in a written notice served on the defendant in accordance with Rule 4 if the complaint seeks an unspecified amount pursuant to Rule 8.01, shall enter judgment for the amount due and costs against the defendant.

(b) In all other cases, the party entitled to a judgment by default shall apply to the court therefor. If a party against whom judgment is sought has appeared in the action, that party shall be served with written notice of the application for judgment at least 14 days prior to the hearing on such application. If the action is one for the recovery of money only, the court shall ascertain, by a reference or otherwise, the amount to which the plaintiff is entitled, and order judgment therefor.

(c) If relief other than the recovery of money is demanded and the taking of an account, or the proof of any fact, is necessary to enable the court to give judgment, it may take or hear the same or order a reference for that purpose, and order judgment accordingly.

(d) When service of the summons has been made by published notice, or by delivery of a copy outside the state, no judgment shall be entered on default until the plaintiff shall have filed a bond, approved by the court, conditioned to abide such order as the court may make concerning restitution of any property collected or obtained by virtue of the judgment in case a defense is thereafter permitted and sustained; provided, that in actions involving the title to real estate or to foreclose mortgages thereon such bond shall not be required.

(e) When judgment is entered in an action upon a promissory note, draft or bill of exchange under the provisions of this rule, such promissory note, draft or bill of exchange shall be filed with the court administrator and made a part of the files of the action.

(Amended effective January 1, 2020.)

Task Force Comment--1991 Adoption

Rule 55.01(e) is derived from Rule 12(c) of the Code of Rules for the District Courts.

The change in subsection (a) is intended to deal with the situation of notice of the amount of judgment sought in those cases where the complaint seeks only an unspecified amount in excess of $50,000 pursuant to Minn. R. Civ. P. 8.01 (rule limits ad damnum clauses for unliquidated damages) and Minnesota Statutes, section 544.36 (1990) (statute providing same limitation).

Advisory Committee Comment—2020 Amendments

Rule 55.01(b) is amended as part of the amendments made to the timing provisions of the rules. These amendments implement the adoption of a standard "day" for counting deadlines under the rules—counting all days regardless of the length of the period and standardizing the time periods, where practicable, to a 7-, 14-, 21- or 28-day schedule. This change to the rule lengths the 3-day notice provision of the rule to 14 days because the 3-day notice period has proven too short to allow a meaningful response from the party receiving notice.

55.02. Plaintiffs; Counterclaimants; Cross-Claimants

This rule is applicable whether the party entitled to judgment by default is a plaintiff, a third-party plaintiff, or a party who has pleaded a cross-claim or counterclaim. In all cases, a judgment by default is subject to the limitations of Rule 54.03.

RULE 56. SUMMARY JUDGMENT

56.01. Motion for Summary Judgment or Partial Summary Judgment

A party may move for summary judgment, identifying each claim or defense—or the part of each claim or defense—on which summary judgment is sought. The court shall grant summary judgment if the movant shows that there is no genuine issue as to any material fact and the movant is entitled to judgment as a matter of law. The court shall state on the record or in a written decision the reasons for granting or denying the motion.

(Amended effective July 1, 2018.)

Advisory Committee Comment--1993 Amendments

The amendment to Rule 56.01 is intended to correct a typographical or grammatical error in the existing rule. No change in meaning or interpretation is intended.

56.02. Time to File a Motion

Service and filing of the motion must comply with the requirements of Rule 115.03 of the General Rules of Practice for the District Courts, provided that in no event shall the motion be served less than 14 days before the time fixed for the hearing. Unless the court orders otherwise, a party may not file a motion for summary judgment more than 30 days after the close of all discovery.

(Amended July 1, 2018.)

56.03. Procedures

(a) Supporting Factual Positions. A party asserting that there is no genuine issue as to any material fact must support the assertion by:

(1) citing to particular parts of materials in the record, including depositions, documents, electronically stored information, affidavits, stipulations (including those made for purposes of the motion only), admissions, interrogatory answers, or other materials; or

(2) showing that the materials cited do not establish the absence or presence of a genuine issue for trial, or that an adverse party cannot produce admissible evidence to support the fact.

(b) Objection That a Fact Is Not Supported by Admissible Evidence. A party may object that the material cited to support or dispute a fact cannot be presented in a form that would be admissible in evidence.

(c) Materials Not Cited. The court need consider only the cited materials, but it may consider other materials in the record.

(d) Affidavits. An affidavit used to support or oppose a motion must be made on personal knowledge, set out facts that would be admissible in evidence, and show that the affiant is competent to testify on the matters stated.

(Amended effective July 1, 2018.)

Advisory Committee Comment--1993 Amendments

The amendment to Rule 56.03 is intended to make clear the relationship between this rule and Minn. Gen. R. Prac. 115. Rule 56.03 includes a strict ten-day notice requirement before a summary judgment motion may be heard. This minimum notice period is mandatory unless waived by the parties. See McAllister v. Independent School

District No. 306, 276 Minn. 549, 149 N.W.2d 81 (1967). The rule is intended to provide protection before claims or defenses are summarily determined by requiring a minimum of ten days' notice.

56.04. When Facts Are Unavailable to the Nonmovant

If a nonmovant shows by affidavit that, for specified reasons, it cannot present facts essential to justify its opposition, the court may:
   (a) defer considering the motion or deny it;
   (b) allow time to obtain affidavits or to take discovery; or
   (c) issue any other appropriate order.

(Amended effective July 1, 2018.)

56.05. Failing to Properly Support or Address a Fact

If a party fails to properly support an assertion of fact or fails to properly address another party's assertion of fact as required by Rule 56.03, the court may:
   (a) give an opportunity to properly support or address the fact;
   (b) consider the fact undisputed for purposes of the motion;
   (c) grant summary judgment if the motion and supporting materials—including the facts considered undisputed—show that the movant is entitled to it; or
   (d) issue any other appropriate order.

(Amended effective July 1, 2018.)

Advisory Committee Comments—2015 Amendments

Rule 56.05 is amended in two ways. The first is not substantive in nature or intended effect. The replacement of "papers" with "documents" is made throughout these rules, and simply advances precision in choice of language. Most documents will not be filed as "paper" documents, so paper is retired as a descriptor of them.

The second change is substantive in nature, and expressly implements a new statute directing the courts to consider accepting documents without notarization if they are signed under the following language: "I declare under penalty of perjury that everything I have stated in this document is true and correct." Minn. Stat. § 358.116 (2014) (codifying 2014 Minn. Laws ch. 204, § 3). The statute allows the courts to require specifically by rule that notarization is necessary, but the difficulty in accomplishing and documenting notarization for documents that are e-filed and e-served militates against requiring formal notarization. Accordingly, summary judgment affidavits may be signed by the party under penalty of perjury, so long as the appropriate language is included above the party's signature. The rule also requires inclusion of the date of signing and the county and state where signed to provide information necessary to establish the fact and venue of possible perjury; this information is otherwise provided by notarization. Rule 15 of the Minnesota General Rules of Practice provides that documents signed in accordance with its terms constitute "affidavits."

56.06. Judgment Independent of the Motion

After giving notice and a reasonable time to respond, the court may:
(a) grant summary judgment for a nonmovant;
(b) grant the motion on grounds not raised by a party; or
(c) consider summary judgment on its own initiative after identifying for the parties the material facts that may not be genuinely in dispute.

(Amended effective July 1, 2018.)

56.07. Failing to Grant All the Requested Relief

If the court does not grant all the relief requested by the motion, it may enter an order stating any material fact—including an item of damages or other relief—that is not genuinely at issue and treating the fact as established in the case.

(Amended effective July 1, 2018.)

56.08. Affidavit Submitted in Bad Faith

If satisfied that an affidavit under this rule is submitted in bad faith or solely for delay, the court—after notice and a reasonable time to respond—may order the submitting party to pay the other party the reasonable expenses, including attorney's fees, it incurred as a result. An offending party or attorney may also be held in contempt or subjected to other appropriate sanctions.

(Amended effective July 1, 2018.)

Advisory Committee Comment—2018 Amendments

Rule 56 is extensively revamped to improve its operation. These amendments closely follow the amendments to Rule 56 of the Federal Rules of Civil Procedure in 2010. They are not intended to change substantially practice under the rule, and very carefully preserve the familiar test of "no genuine issue as to any material fact and the movant is entitled to judgment as a matter of law" in Rule 56.01.

Rule 56.03(c) makes it clear that the court is not required to consider any matters beyond those filed in conjunction with the motion for summary judgment—filed by either the movant or any other parties. Rule 115.03(d) of the Minnesota General Rules of Practice sets forth specific requirements for what must be filed for summary judgment motions and responses. Rule 56.03 also retains, however, the traditional rule allowing the court to base either the grant or denial of summary judgment on any factual material contained in the record—this means the entire court file record, including all pleadings, other filings, and transcripts of arguments or hearings.

Rule 56.03(d) refers to "affidavits" as that term is defined for all proceedings by Rule 15 of the Minnesota General Rules of Practice. That rule encompasses both statements signed, sworn to, and notarized and statements signed under penalty of perjury in accordance with the rule.

Rule 56.06 carries forward the existing procedure allowing entry of judgment in favor of the movant or nonmovant, granting the motion on grounds other than those argued, or considering summary judgment on its own initiative. See, e.g., Del Hayes & Sons, Inc. v Mitchell, 304 Minn. 275, 230 N.W.2d 588 (1975) (sua sponte grant of summary judgment allowed). Where the court acts on its own initiative, the rule specifies that the parties are entitled to notice of its view about fact issues that may not be in dispute. That notice should precede any order for summary judgment by the 14-day minimum notice period specified in Rule 56.02.

RULE 57. DECLARATORY JUDGMENTS

The procedure for obtaining a declaratory judgment pursuant to Minnesota Statutes, chapter 555, shall be in accordance with these rules, and the right to trial by jury is retained under the circumstances and in the manner provided in Rules 38 and 39. The existence of another adequate remedy does not preclude a judgment for declaratory relief in cases where it is appropriate. The court may order a speedy hearing of an action for a declaratory judgment and may advance it on the calendar.

RULE 58. ENTRY OF JUDGMENT; STAY

58.01. Entry

Unless the court otherwise directs, and subject to the provisions of Rule 54.02, judgment upon the verdict of a jury, or upon an order of the court for the recovery of money only or for costs or that all relief be denied, shall be entered forthwith by the court administrator; but the court shall direct the appropriate judgment to be entered upon a special verdict or upon a general verdict accompanied by answers to interrogatories returned by a jury pursuant to Rule 49 or upon an order of the court for relief other than money or costs. Entry of judgment shall not be delayed for the taxation of costs, and the omission of costs shall not affect the finality of the judgment. The judgment in all cases shall be entered and signed by the court administrator in the judgment roll; this entry constitutes the entry of the judgment; and the judgment is not effective before such entry.

58.02. Stay

The court may order a stay of entry of judgment upon a verdict or decision for a period not exceeding the time required for the hearing and determination of a motion for new trial or for judgment notwithstanding the verdict or to set the verdict aside or to dismiss the action or for amended findings, and after such determination may order a stay of entry of judgment for not more than 30 days. In granting a stay of entry of judgment pursuant to this rule for any period exceeding 30 days after verdict or decision, the court, in its discretion, may impose such conditions for the security of the adverse party as may be deemed proper.

RULE 59. NEW TRIALS

59.01. Grounds

A new trial may be granted to all or any of the parties and on all or part of the issues for any of the following causes:

(a) Irregularity in the proceedings of the court, referee, jury, or prevailing party, or any order or abuse of discretion, whereby the moving party was deprived of a fair trial;

(b) Misconduct of the jury or prevailing party;

(c) Accident or surprise which could not have been prevented by ordinary prudence;

(d) Material evidence newly discovered, which with reasonable diligence could not have been found and produced at the trial;

(e) Excessive or insufficient damages, appearing to have been given under the influence of passion or prejudice;

(f) Errors of law occurring at the trial, and objected to at the time or, if no objection need have been made pursuant to Rules 46 and 51, plainly assigned in the notice of motion;

(g) The verdict, decision, or report is not justified by the evidence, or is contrary to law; but, unless it be so expressly stated in the order granting a new trial, it shall not be presumed, on appeal, to have been made on the ground that the verdict, decision, or report was not justified by the evidence.

On a motion for a new trial in an action tried without a jury, the court may open the judgment if one has been entered, take additional testimony, amend findings of fact and conclusions of law or make new findings and conclusions, and direct entry of a new judgment.

59.02. Basis of Motion

A motion made pursuant to Rule 59.01 shall be made and heard on the files, exhibits, and minutes of the court. Pertinent facts that would not be a part of the minutes may be shown by affidavit. A full or partial transcript of the court reporter's notes may be used on the hearing of the motion.

59.03. Time for Motion

A notice of motion for a new trial shall be served within 30 days after a general verdict or service of notice by a party of the filing of the decision or order; and the motion shall be heard within 60 days after such general verdict or notice of filing, unless the time for hearing be extended by the court within the 60-day period for good cause shown.

Advisory Committee Comment--2000 Amendments

The single purpose of the amendment of this Rule 59.03 in 2000 is to create a longer and more reasonable period in which to hear post-trial motions. At the time this rule was adopted, post-trial motions were often heard in a somewhat perfunctory manner and court assignment practices permitted the scheduling of cases in this manner.

This amendment will also reduce, although not eliminate, the potential consequences of failing to have a post-trial motion heard in a timely manner.

The change in Rule 59 will serve to extend the deadline for other post-trial motions as well, because the current rules specifically tie the deadlines for those motions to Rule 59. See MINN. R. CIV. P. 50.02(c) (judgment notwithstanding the verdict); 52.02 (motion for amended findings). It will also have an indirect impact on Rule 60.02(b), which allows for relief from an order or judgment on the grounds of newly discovered evidence which could not have been discovered in time to move for a new trial. This latter impact will be negligible.

59.04. Time for Serving Affidavits

When a motion for a new trial is based upon affidavits, they shall be served with the notice of motion. The opposing party shall have 14 days after such service in which to serve opposing affidavits, which period may be extended by the court pursuant to Rule 59.03. The court may permit reply affidavits.

(Amended effective January 1, 2020.)

59.05. On Initiative of Court

Not later than 14 days after a general verdict or the filing of the decision or order, the court upon its own initiative may order a new trial for any reason for which it might have granted a new trial on motion of a party. After giving the parties notice and an opportunity to be heard on the matter, the court may grant a motion for a new trial, timely served, for a reason not stated in the motion. In either case, the court shall specify in the order the grounds therefor.

(Amended effective January 1, 2020.)

59.06. Stay of Entry of Judgment

A stay of entry of judgment pursuant to Rule 58 shall not be construed to extend the time within which a party may serve a motion hereunder.

Advisory Committee Comment—2020 Amendments

Rules 59.04 and 59.05 are amended as part of the extensive amendments made to the timing provisions of the rules. These amendments implement the adoption of a standard "day" for counting deadlines under the rules—counting all days regardless of the length of the period and standardizing the time periods, where practicable, to a 7-, 14-, 21- or 28-day schedule. The only change to Rule 59.04 changes the 10-day period for serving opposing affidavits to 14 days. The only change to Rule 59.05 changes the 15-day period for issue a court initiated new trial to 14 days. These changes affect only the time limits, and are not intended to have any other effect.

RULE 60. RELIEF FROM JUDGMENT OR ORDER

60.01. Clerical Mistakes

Clerical mistakes in judgments, orders, or other parts of the record and errors therein arising from oversight or omission may be corrected by the court at any time upon its own initiative or on the motion of any party and after such notice, if any, as the court orders. During the pendency of an appeal, such mistakes may be so corrected with leave of the appellate court.

60.02. Mistakes; Inadvertence; Excusable Neglect; Newly Discovered Evidence; Fraud; etc.

On motion and upon such terms as are just, the court may relieve a party or the party's legal representatives from a final judgment (other than a marriage dissolution decree), order, or proceeding and may order a new trial or grant such other relief as may be just for the following reasons:

- (a) Mistake, inadvertence, surprise, or excusable neglect;
- (b) Newly discovered evidence which by due diligence could not have been discovered in time to move for a new trial pursuant to Rule 59.03;
- (c) Fraud (whether heretofore denominated intrinsic or extrinsic), misrepresentation, or other misconduct of an adverse party;
- (d) The judgment is void;
- (e) The judgment has been satisfied, released, or discharged or a prior judgment upon which it is based has been reversed or otherwise vacated, or it is no longer equitable that the judgment should have prospective application; or
- (f) Any other reason justifying relief from the operation of the judgment.

The motion shall be made within a reasonable time, and for reasons (a), (b), and (c) not more than one year after the judgment, order, or proceeding was entered or taken. A Rule 60.02 motion does not affect the finality of a judgment or suspend its operation. This rule does not limit the power of a court to entertain an independent action to relieve a party from a judgment, order, or proceeding, or to grant relief to a defendant not actually personally notified as provided in Rule 4.043, or to set aside a judgment for fraud upon the court. Writs of coram nobis, coram vobis, audita querela, and bills of review and bills in the nature of a bill of review are abolished, and the procedure for obtaining any relief from a judgment shall be by motion as prescribed in these rules or by an independent action.

(Amended effective March 1, 1994.)

Advisory Committee Comment--1993 Amendments

The only change made to this rule is to correct the reference to marriage dissolution as that is the current name for the proceeding. This amendment is intended to be consistent with similar amendments to the rules made in 1988.

RULE 61. HARMLESS ERROR

No error in either the admission or the exclusion of evidence and no error or defect in any ruling or order or in anything done or omitted by the court or by any of the parties is ground for granting a new trial or for setting aside a verdict or for vacating, modifying, or otherwise disturbing a judgment or order, unless refusal to take such action appears to the court inconsistent with substantial justice. The court at every stage of the proceeding must disregard any error or defect in the proceeding which does not affect the substantial rights of the parties.

RULE 62. STAY OF PROCEEDINGS TO ENFORCE A JUDGMENT

62.01. Stay on Motions

In its discretion and on such conditions for the security of the adverse party as are proper, the court may stay the execution of or any proceedings to enforce a judgment pending the disposition of a motion for a new trial made pursuant to Rule 59, or of a motion for relief from a judgment or order made pursuant to Rule 60, or of a motion for judgment as a matter of law made pursuant to Rule 50.02, or of a motion for amendment to the findings or for additional findings made pursuant to Rule 52.02.

Advisory Committee Comment—2006 Amendment

Rule 62.01 is amended to reflect the new name for motions under Rule 50.01 as amended effective January 1, 2006.

62.02. Injunction Pending Appeal

When an appeal is taken from an interlocutory or final judgment granting, dissolving, or denying an injunction, the court in its discretion may suspend, modify, restore, or grant an injunction during the pendency of the appeal upon such terms as to bond or otherwise as it considers proper for the security of the rights of the adverse party.

62.03. Stay Upon Appeal

When an appeal is taken, the appellant may obtain a stay only when authorized and in the manner provided in Rules 107 and 108, Rules of Civil Appellate Procedure.

62.04. Stay in Favor of the State or Agency Thereof

When an appeal is taken by the state or an officer, agency, or governmental subdivision thereof, and the operation or enforcement of the judgment is stayed, no bond, obligation, or other security shall be required from the appellant.

62.05. Power of Appellate Court Not Limited

The provisions of Rule 62 do not limit any power of an appellate court or of a judge or justice thereof to stay proceedings during the pendency of an appeal or to suspend, modify, restore, or grant an injunction during the pendency of an appeal or to make any order appropriate to preserve the status quo or the effectiveness of the judgment subsequently to be entered.

62.06. Stay of Judgment Upon Multiple Claims

When a court has ordered a final judgment on some but not all of the claims presented in the action under the conditions stated in Rule 54.02, the court may stay enforcement of that judgment until the entering of a subsequent judgment or judgments and may prescribe such conditions as are necessary to secure the benefits thereof to the party in whose favor the judgment is entered.

RULE 63. DISABILITY OR DISQUALIFICATION OF JUDGE; NOTICE TO REMOVE; ASSIGNMENT OF A JUDGE

63.01. Disability of Judge

If by reason of death, sickness, or other disability a judge before whom an action has been tried is unable to perform judicial duties after a verdict is returned or findings of fact and conclusions of law are filed, any other judge regularly sitting in or assigned to the court in which the action was tried may perform those duties; but if such other judge is satisfied that the duties cannot be performed because that judge did not preside at the trial or for any other reason, that judge may exercise discretion to grant a new trial.

63.02. Interest or Bias

No judge shall sit in any case if disqualified under the Code of Judicial Conduct. If there is no other judge of the district who is qualified, or if there is only one judge of the district, such judge shall forthwith notify the chief justice of the supreme court of that judge's disqualification.

(Amended effective July 1, 2018.)

63.03. Notice to Remove

Any party or attorney may make and serve on the opposing party and file with the administrator a notice to remove. The notice shall be served and filed within ten days after the party receives notice of which judge or judicial officer is to preside at the trial or hearing, but not later than the commencement of the trial or hearing.

No such notice may be filed by a party or party's attorney against a judge or judicial officer who has presided at a motion or any other proceeding of which the party had notice, or who is assigned by the Chief Justice of the Minnesota Supreme Court. A judge or judicial officer who has presided at a motion or other proceeding or who is assigned by the Chief Justice of the Minnesota Supreme Court may not be removed except upon an affirmative showing that the judge or judicial officer is disqualified under the Code of Judicial Conduct.

After a party has once disqualified a presiding judge or judicial officer as a matter of right that party may disqualify the substitute judge or judicial officer, but only by making an affirmative showing that the judge or judicial officer is disqualified under the Code of Judicial Conduct.

Upon the filing of a notice to remove or if a litigant makes an affirmative showing that a substitute judge or judicial officer is disqualified under the code of Judicial Conduct, the chief judge of the judicial district shall assign any other judge of any court within the district, or a judicial officer in the case of a substitute judicial officer, to hear the cause.

(Amended effective July 1, 2018.)

Task Force Comment--1991 Adoption

This amendment to Minn. R. Civ. P. 63.03 is intended to provide a uniform mechanism for removing any judicial officer, whether a judge or referee. This rule would replace various inconsistent provisions of the existing rules. 4th Dist. R. 16.01 requires objections to any referee to be filed one court day before the hearing. 2d Dist. R. 23 requires objection within 10 days after notice of assignment and not later than commencement, consistent with the statute and rule governing judges.

Advisory Committee Comments--2000 Amendments

Rule 63.03 is amended to make clear the fact that a judge specially assigned by the Chief Justice to hear cases originally pending in more than one district cannot be removed by mere filing of a notice to remove. This amendment is a companion to the amendment of Rule 113.03 of the Minnesota General Rules of Practice in 2000, effective March 1, 2001, to provide a formal mechanism for requesting the Chief Justice to make such an assignment. This rule codifies the existing practice in special cases such as special assignment of a judge by the Chief Justice. The rule makes it clear that even a judge assigned by the Chief Justice may be removed for cause.

Advisory Committee Comment—2018 Amendments

Rule 63 is amended to apply the disqualification standard of the Minnesota Code of Judicial Conduct to disqualification under the civil rules. The standard in the existing rule—whether the judicial officer would be excused from service as a juror and tying that determination to an affirmative showing of prejudice—does not accurately state the correct standard. Rule 26.03, subd. 14(3) of the Minnesota Rules of Criminal Procedure uses the Code of Judicial Conduct standard, and the Minnesota Supreme Court has applied the Code of Judicial Conduct for deciding questions of disqualification of judges on the Minnesota Court of Appeals. See Powell v. Anderson, 660 N.W.2d 107, 114–15 (Minn. 2003). The juror-based standard dates back to Minnesota's Territorial days. See Minn. Rev. Stat. 1851, ch. 69, art. 2, § 5. The standard has not been modified in the civil rules since, including upon the adoption of the Code of Judicial Conduct by the Minnesota Supreme Court in 1974.

This amended rule adopts a standard for disqualification or recusal of a judge that is clearer and readily accessible to judges and litigants. Although close questions of disqualification may properly be resolved in favor of disqualification, the Code of Judicial Conduct also recognizes that a judicial officer has an affirmative duty to hear matters properly assigned where disqualification is not required by the Code. See Rule 2.7 of the Code of Judicial Conduct.

63.04. Assignment of Judge

Upon receiving notice as provided in Rules 63.02 and 63.03, the chief justice shall assign a judge of another district, accepting such assignment, to preside at the trial or hearing, and the trial or hearing shall be postponed until the judge so assigned can be present.

VII. PROVISIONAL AND FINAL REMEDIES AND SPECIAL PROCEEDINGS

RULE 64. SEIZURE OF PERSON OR PROPERTY

At the commencement of and during the course of an action, all remedies providing for seizure of person or property for the purpose of securing satisfaction of the judgment ultimately to be entered in the action are available under the circumstances and in the manner provided by the law of the state.

RULE 65. INJUNCTIONS

65.01. Temporary Restraining Order; Notice; Hearing; Duration

A temporary restraining order may be granted without written or oral notice to the adverse party or that party's attorney only if (1) it clearly appears from specific facts shown by affidavit or by the verified complaint that immediate and irreparable injury, loss, or damage will result to the applicant before the adverse party or that party's attorney can be heard in opposition, and (2) the applicant's attorney states to the court in writing the efforts, if any, which have been made to give notice or the reasons supporting the claim that notice should not be required. In the event that a temporary restraining order is based upon any affidavit, a copy of such affidavit must be served with the temporary restraining order. In case a temporary restraining order is granted without notice, the motion for a temporary injunction shall be set down for hearing at the earliest practicable time and shall take precedence over all matters except older matters of the same character; and when the motion comes on for hearing, the party who obtained the temporary restraining order shall proceed with the application for a temporary injunction, and, if the party does not do so, the court shall dissolve the temporary restraining order. On written or oral notice to the party who obtained the ex parte temporary restraining order, the adverse party may appear and move its dissolution or modification, and in that event the court shall proceed to hear and determine such motion as expeditiously as the ends of justice require.

65.02. Temporary Injunction

(a) No temporary injunction shall be granted without notice of motion or an order to show cause to the adverse party.

(b) A temporary injunction may be granted if by affidavit, deposition testimony, or oral testimony in court, it appears that sufficient grounds exist therefor.

(c) Before or after the commencement of the hearing on a motion for a temporary injunction, the court may order the trial of the action on the merits to be advanced and consolidated with the hearing on the motion. Even when this consolidation is not ordered, any evidence received upon a motion for a temporary injunction which would be admissible at the trial on the merits becomes part of the trial record and need not be repeated at trial. This provision shall be so construed and applied as to preserve any rights the parties may have to trial by jury.

65.03. Security

(a) No temporary restraining order or temporary injunction shall be granted except upon the giving of security by the applicant, in such sum as the court deems proper, for the payment of such costs and damages as may be incurred or suffered by any party who is found to have been wrongfully enjoined or restrained.

(b) Whenever security is given in the form of a bond or other undertaking with one or more sureties, each surety submits to the jurisdiction of the court and irrevocably appoints the court administrator as the surety's agent upon whom any documents affecting liability on the bond or undertaking may be served. The surety's liability may be enforced on motion without the necessity of an independent action. The motion and such notice of the motion as the court prescribes may be served on the court administrator, who shall forthwith transmit copies to the sureties if their addresses are known.

(Amended effective July 1, 2015.)

Advisory Committee Comments—2015 Amendments

The amendments to Rule 65.03 are not substantive in nature or intended effect. The replacement of "papers" with "documents" is made throughout these rules, and simply advances precision in choice of language. Most documents will not be filed as "paper" documents, so paper is retired as a descriptor of them. The word "transmit" is used in preference to "mail," recognizing that many documents will be delivered by electronic or means other than the United States mail.

65.04. Form and Scope of Injunction or Restraining Order

Every order granting an injunction and every restraining order shall set forth the reasons for its issuance; shall be specific in terms; shall describe in reasonable detail, and not by reference to the complaint or other document, the act or acts sought to be restrained; and is binding only upon the parties to the action, their officers, agents, servants, employees, and attorneys, and upon those persons in active concert or participation with them who receive actual notice of the order by personal service or otherwise.

Advisory Committee Comments--2000 Amendments

This rule is entirely new in the Minnesota rules; it is drawn directly from FED. R. CIV. P. 65(d). There is no comparable provision currently in the Minnesota rules and questions do arise about what is necessary to make sure that a party is subject to a court's injunctive order. The amended rule is intended to resolve those questions.

RULE 66. RECEIVERS

An action wherein a receiver has been appointed shall not be dismissed except by order of the court. A foreign receiver shall have capacity to sue in any district court, but the receiver's rights are subordinate to those of local creditors. The practice in the administration of estates by the court shall be in accordance with Minnesota Statutes, chapter 576 and with the practice heretofore followed in the courts of this state or as provided in rules promulgated by the district courts. In all other respects, the action in which the appointment of a receiver is sought or which is brought by or against a receiver is governed by these rules.

RULE 67. DEPOSIT IN COURT

67.01. In an Action

In an action in which any part of the relief sought is a judgment for a sum of money or the disposition of a sum of money or the disposition of any other thing capable of delivery, a party, upon notice to every other party, and by leave of court, may deposit with the court all or any part of such money or thing.

67.02. When No Action is Brought

When money or other personal property in the possession of any person, as bailee or otherwise, is claimed adversely by two or more other persons, and the right thereto as between such claimants is in doubt, the person in possession, though no action is commenced against that person by any of the claimants, may place the property in the custody of the court. The person in possession shall apply to the court of the county in which the property is situated, setting forth by petition the facts which bring the case within the provisions of this rule, and the names and places of residence of all known claimants of such property. If satisfied of the truth of such showing, the court, by order, shall accept custody of the money or other property, and direct that, upon delivery and upon giving notice thereof to all persons interested, personally or by certified mail as prescribed in such order, the petitioner is relieved from further liability on account thereof. This rule shall apply to cases where property held under like conditions is garnished in the hands of the possessor; but in such cases the application shall be made to the court in which the garnishment proceedings are pending.

(Amended effective September 1, 2020.)

Advisory Committee Comment-2020 Amendments
Rule 67.02 is amended to remove the requirement that notice by mail be given by registered mail. The archaic specification of mailing by registered mail imposes only additional expense. Use of certified mail provides a record of the actual delivery, which is what is needed for the notice under this rule. The court may, but need not, require that delivery be restricted to the particular person or entity entitled to notice. A party serving notice under the rule may use certified mail with return receipt requested in order to obtain evidence of receipt, and may have the postal service restrict delivery to a particular individual. If service is to be made pursuant to the Hague Convention on the Service Abroad of Judicial and Extrajudicial Documents, as allowed under Rule 4.04(c)(1), a different form of service may be required.

67.03. Court May Order Deposit or Seizure of Property

When it is admitted by the pleading or examination of a party that the party has possession or control of any money or other thing capable of delivery which, being the subject of the litigation, is held by that party as trustee for another party, or which belongs or is due to another party, the court may order the same to be deposited in court or delivered to such other party, with or without security, subject to further direction. If such order is disobeyed, the court may punish the disobedience as a contempt, and may also require the sheriff or other proper officer to take the money or property and deposit or deliver it in accordance with the direction given.

67.04. Money Paid into Court

Where money is paid into the court pending the result of any legal proceedings, the judge may order it deposited in a bank account maintained by the court administrator.

(Amended effective July 1, 2018.)

> **Advisory Committee Comment—2018 Amendments**
> *Rule 67.04 is amended to reflect the abrogation of the statutory bond requirement for court administrators found in the prior version of the rule. See 2006 Minn. Laws, ch. 260, art 5, § 40. Because of that legislative change, the rule is amended to allow deposit in court by order of the court. The court can determine the appropriate terms for that deposit. As a practical matter, an order is necessary to authorize the administrator to accept the funds and to provide for release of the funds upon further order.*

RULE 68. OFFER OF JUDGMENT OR SETTLEMENT

Rule 68.01. Offer.

(a) **Time of Offer.** At any time more than 14 days before the trial begins, any party may serve upon an adverse party a written damages-only or total-obligation offer to allow judgment to be entered to the effect specified in the offer, or to settle the case on the terms specified in the offer.

(b) **Applicability of Rule.** An offer does not have the consequences provided in Rules 68.02 and 68.03 unless it expressly refers to Rule 68.

(c) **Damages-only Offers.** An offer made under this rule is a "damages-only" offer unless the offer expressly states that it is a "total-obligation" offer. A damages-only offer does not include then-accrued applicable prejudgment interest, costs and disbursements, or applicable attorney fees, all of which shall be added to the amount stated as provided in Rules 68.02(b)(2) and (c).

(d) **Total-obligation Offers.** The amount stated in an offer that is expressly identified as a "total-obligation" offer includes then-accrued applicable prejudgment interest, costs and disbursements, and applicable attorney fees.

(e) **Offer Following Determination of Liability.** When the liability of one party to another has been determined by verdict, order, or judgment, but the amount or extent of the liability remains to be determined by further proceedings, the party adjudged liable may make an offer of judgment, which shall have the same effect as an offer made before trial if it is served within a reasonable time not less than 14 days before the commencement of a hearing or trial to determine the amount or extent of liability.

(f) **Filing.** Notwithstanding the provisions of Rule 5.04, no offer under this rule need be filed with the court unless the offer is accepted.

(Amended effective January 1, 2020.)

Rule 68.02. Acceptance or Rejection of Offer.

(a) **Time for Acceptance.** Acceptance of the offer shall be made by service of written notice of acceptance within 14 days after service of the offer. During the 14-day period the offer is irrevocable.

(b) **Effect of Acceptance of Offer of Judgment.** If the offer accepted is an offer of judgment, either party may file the offer and the notice of acceptance, together with the proof of service thereof, and the court shall order entry of judgment as follows:

   (1) If the offer is a total-obligation offer as provided in Rule 68.01(d), judgment shall be for the amount of the offer.
   (2) If the offer is a damages-only offer, applicable prejudgment interest, the plaintiff-offeree's costs and disbursements, and applicable attorney fees, all as accrued to the date of the offer, shall be determined by the court and included in the judgment.

(c) **Effect of Acceptance of Offer of Settlement.** If the offer accepted is an offer of settlement, the settled claim(s) shall be dismissed upon
   (1) the filing of a stipulation of dismissal stating that the terms of the offer, including payment of applicable prejudgment interest, costs and disbursements, and applicable attorney fees, all accrued to the date of the offer, have been satisfied or
   (2) order of the court implementing the terms of the agreement.

(d) **Offer Deemed Withdrawn.** If the offer is not accepted within the 14-day period, it shall be deemed withdrawn.

(e) **Subsequent Offers.** The fact that an offer is made but not accepted does not preclude a subsequent offer. Any subsequent offer by the same party under this rule supersedes all prior offers by that party.

(Amended effective January 1, 2020.)

Rule 68.03. Effect of Unaccepted Offer.

(a) **Unaccepted Offer Not Admissible.** Evidence of an unaccepted offer is not admissible, except in a proceeding to determine costs and disbursements.

(b) **Effect of Offer on Recovery of Costs.** An unaccepted offer affects the parties' obligations and entitlements regarding costs and disbursements as follows:

(1) If the offeror is a defendant, and the defendant-offeror prevails or the relief awarded to the plaintiff-offeree is less favorable than the offer, the plaintiff-offeree must pay the defendant-offeror's costs and disbursements incurred in the defense of the action after service of the offer, and the plaintiff-offeree shall not recover its costs and disbursements incurred after service of the offer, provided that applicable attorney fees available to the plaintiff-offeree shall not be affected by this provision.

(2) If the offeror is a plaintiff, and the relief awarded is less favorable to the defendant-offeree than the offer, the defendant-offeree must pay, in addition to the costs and disbursements to which the plaintiff-offeror is entitled under Rule 54.04, an amount equal to the plaintiff-offeror's costs and disbursements incurred after service of the offer. Applicable attorney fees available to the plaintiff-offeror shall not be affected by this provision.

(3) If the court determines that the obligations imposed under this rule as a result of a party's failure to accept an offer would impose undue hardship or otherwise be inequitable, the court may reduce the amount of the obligations to eliminate the undue hardship or inequity.

(c) **Measuring Result Compared to Offer.** To determine for purposes of this rule if the relief awarded is less favorable to the offeree than the offer:
(1) a damages-only offer is compared with the amount of damages awarded to the plaintiff; and
(2) a total-obligation offer is compared with the amount of damages awarded to the plaintiff, plus applicable prejudgment interest, the plaintiff's taxable costs and disbursements, and applicable attorney fees, all as accrued to the date of the offer.

Rule 68.04. Applicable Attorney Fees and Prejudgment Interest.

(a) **"Applicable Attorney Fees" Defined.** "Applicable attorney fees" for purposes of Rule 68 means any attorney fees to which a party is entitled by statute, common law, or contract for one or more of the claims resolved by an offer made under the rule. Nothing in this rule shall be construed to create a right to attorney fees not provided for under the applicable substantive law.

(b) **"Applicable Prejudgment Interest" Defined.** "Applicable prejudgment interest" for purposes of Rule 68 means any prejudgment interest to which a party is entitled by statute, rule, common law, or contract for one or more of the claims resolved by an offer made under the rule. Nothing in this rule shall be construed to create a right to prejudgment interest not provided for under the applicable substantive law.

(Amended effective July 1, 2008.)

Advisory Committee Comment—2008 Amendment

Rule 68 is extensively revamped both to clarify its operation and to make it more effective in its purpose of encouraging the settlement of litigation. The overarching goal of this set of amendments is to add certainty to the operation of the rule and to remove surprises both to parties making offers and those receiving and deciding whether to accept them. Additionally, Rule 68.03 is revised to make the mechanism of Rule 68 better address the goal of providing incentives for both claimants and parties opposing claims. This rule is not as closely modeled on its federal counterpart, Fed. R. Civ. P. 68, as is the existing rule, so that rule and decisions construing it may not be persuasive guidance in construing this rule.

Rule 68 uses the term "offer" to include offers to settle made by any party. Thus, both an offer by a defendant to pay a sum in return for a dismissal of a claim and an offer by a claimant to accept a sum in return for dismissal—often termed a "demand" and not an "offer"—are offers for the purposes of the rule.

Rule 68.01(b) is a new provision that requires that in order to be given the cost-shifting effect of the rule an offer must include express reference to the rule. See Matheiu v. Freeman, 472 N.W.2d 187 (Minn. App. 1991). This provision is intended to make it unlikely that an offer would come within the scope of the rule without the offeror intending that and the offeree having notice that it is an offer with particular consequences as defined in the rule.

The revised rule carries forward the former rule's application both to offers of judgment and to offers of settlement. The effects of these two types of offer are different, and are clarified in Rule 68.02. Rules 68.01(c) and (d) create an additional dichotomy in the rule, creating new categories of "damages-only" and "total-obligation" offers. This dichotomy is important to the operation of the rule, and is intended to remove a significant "trap for the unwary" where an accepted offer may be given two substantially different interpretations by offeror and offeree. Under the former rule, if a statute allowed the recovery of attorney fees as costs and a Rule 68 offer were made and did not expressly include reference to attorney fees, fees could be recovered in addition to the amount offered. See, e.g., Collins v. Minn. Sch. of Business, Inc., 655 N.W.2d 320 (Minn. 2003). Fees recoverable by contract, rather than statute, would be subsumed within the offer, and not be recoverable in addition to the amount of the accepted offer. See, e.g., Schwickert, Inc. v. Winnebago Seniors, Ltd., 680 N.W.2d 79 (Minn. 2004). Similar uncertainty may exist as to whether prejudgment interest is included in or to be added to the amount of an offer. See, e.g., Collins; Stinson v. Clark Equip. Co., 743 N.W.2d 333 (Minn. App. 1991). Discussion of other ambiguities under the federal counterpart to Rule 68, Fed. R. Civ. P. 68, is included in Danielle M. Shelton, Rewriting Rule 68: Realizing the Benefits of the Federal Settlement Rule by Injecting Certainty into Offers of Judgment, 91 Minn. L. Rev. 865 (2007).

The "damages-only" or "total obligation" offer choice allows the party making the offer to control and understand the effect of the offer, if accepted; similarly, a party deciding how to respond to an offer should be able to determine the total cost of accepting an offer. Rule 68.01(c) creates a presumption that an offer made under Rule 68 is a "damages-only" offer unless it expressly meets the criteria of Rule 68.01(d) by stating that it is a "total-obligation" offer. The added precision allowed by distinguishing the types of offers permits the new rule to provide greater clarity and certainty as to the effect both of accepted offers and unaccepted offers.

Rule 68.03(b)(1) changes the effect of Rule 68 on costs and disbursements when a defendant's offer is rejected and the judgment is less favorable to the plaintiff offeree. Under the former rule, the offeree would nevertheless recover its costs and disbursements from the offeror. Borchert v. Maloney, 581 N.W.2d 838 (Minn. 1998). The revised rule provides that the offeree does not recover its costs and disbursements incurred after service of the offer. But this change does not affect a prevailing plaintiff's right to attorney fees to which it is entitled under law or contract. In this respect the revised rule, like the former rule, does not incorporate the cut-off of attorney fees that occurs under the federal Rule 68 as interpreted in Marek v. Chesney, 473 U.S. 1 (1986). Additionally, under the former rule, the offeror was entitled to its costs and disbursements incurred from the beginning of the case. Vandenheuvel v. Wagner, 690 N.W.2d 757 (Minn. 2005). As to this issue, the revised rule now has the same effect as the federal rule (although with language that is not identical), requiring the offeree to pay the offeror's costs and disbursements incurred after service of the offer.

Rule 68.03(b)(2) introduces a consequence for a defendant's rejection of a plaintiff's Rule 68 offer if the judgment is less favorable to the defendant offeree. In that circumstance, this new provision requires the defendant to pay double the offeror's costs and disbursements incurred after service of the offer. If the defendant is merely required to pay the offeror's costs, as under the current rule, there is no adverse consequence for a defendant who rejects a Rule 68 offer. In contrast, under the revised rule, a plaintiff who rejects a Rule 68 offer suffers dual adverse consequences: loss of the right to recover his costs and required payment of the defendant's costs.

Rule 68.04(a) expressly provides that the rule does not create a right to recover attorney fees. This provision is intended only to avoid confusion. The rule might affect the extent of fees recoverable by statute, common law, or by contract, but it does not create any right to recover fees that does not exist outside of Rule 68.

Similarly, Rule 68.04(b) provides that the rule does not create a right to prejudgment interest, which right must rather be drawn from an applicable statute, rule, contract, or common law. It is noteworthy that Minn. Stat. § 549.09, subd. 1(b), which governs prejudgment interest in most cases, contains a mechanism analogous to this rule that adjusts calculation of prejudgment interest based on the relationship between the parties' offers of settlement and the ultimate judgment or award in the case.

Advisory Committee Comment—2020 Amendments

Rules 68.01, 68.02(a) & (d) are amended as part of the amendments made to the timing provisions of the rules. These amendments implement the adoption of a standard "day" for counting deadlines under the rules—counting all days regardless of the length of the period and standardizing the time periods, where practicable, to a 7-, 14-, 21- or 28-day schedule. The only change to Rule 68.01 extends the time to make an offer of judgment from 10 days before trial begins to 14 days before trial begins. The change to Rule 68.02 extends the time to respond to an offer of judgment from 10 days to 14 days. These changes affect only the time limits, and are not intended to have any other effect.

RULE 69. EXECUTION

Process to enforce a judgment for the payment of money shall be a writ of execution, unless the court directs otherwise. The procedure on execution, in proceedings supplementary to and in aid of a judgment, and in proceedings on and in aid of execution shall be in accordance with Minnesota Statutes, chapter 550. In aid of the judgment or execution, the judgment creditor, or successor in interest when that interest appears of record, may obtain discovery from any person, including the judgment debtor, in the manner provided by these rules.

RULE 70. JUDGMENT FOR SPECIFIC ACTS; VESTING TITLE

If a judgment directs a party to execute a conveyance of land or to deliver deeds or other documents or to perform any other specific act and the party fails to comply within the time specified, the court may direct the act to be done at the cost of the disobedient party by some other person appointed by the court, and the act when so done has like effect as if done by the party. On application of the party entitled to performance, the court administrator shall issue a writ of attachment against the property of the disobedient party to compel obedience to the judgment. The court may also in proper cases adjudge the party in contempt. If real or personal property is within the state, the court, in lieu of directing a conveyance thereof, may enter a judgment divesting the title of any party and vesting it in others; and such judgment has the effect of a conveyance executed in due form of law. When any order or judgment is for the delivery of possession, the party in whose favor it is entered is entitled to a writ of execution upon application to the court administrator.

RULE 71. PROCESS IN BEHALF OF AND AGAINST PERSONS NOT PARTIES

When an order is made in favor of a person who is not a party to the action, that person may enforce obedience to the order by the same process as if a party; and, when obedience to an order may be lawfully enforced against a person who is not a party, that person is liable to the same process for enforcing obedience to the order as if that person were a party.

RULES 72 TO 76. (RESERVED FOR FUTURE USE.)

VIII. DISTRICT COURTS AND COURT ADMINISTRATORS

RULE 77. DISTRICT COURTS AND COURT ADMINISTRATORS

77.01. District Courts Always Open

The district courts shall be deemed always open for the purpose of filing any pleading or other proper documents, of issuing and returning mesne and final process, and of making and directing all interlocutory motions, orders, and rules.

(Amended effective July 1, 2015.)

77.02. Trials and Hearings; Orders in Chambers

All trials upon the merits shall be conducted in open court and so far as convenient in a regular courtroom. All other acts or proceedings may be done or conducted by a judge in chambers, without the attendance of the court administrator or other court officials and at any place either within or outside the district; but no hearing, other than one ex parte, shall be conducted outside the district without the consent of all parties affected thereby.

77.03. Court Administrator's Office and Orders by Court Administrator

All motions and applications in the court administrator's office for issuing mesne process, for issuing final process to enforce and execute judgments, for entering judgments by default, and for other proceedings which do not require allowance or order of the court are grantable of course by the court administrator; but the court administrator's action may be suspended, altered, or rescinded by the court upon cause shown.

77.04. Notice of Orders or Judgments

Immediately upon the filing of an order or decision or entry of a judgment, the court administrator shall transmit a notice of the filing or entry by mail, e-mail, or by use of an e-filing and e-service system, to every party affected thereby or upon such party's attorney of record, whether or not such party has appeared in the action, at the party or attorney's last known mail or e-mail address, and shall make note the transmission in the court records. Notice under this rule shall not limit the time for taking an appeal or other proceeding on such order, decision, or judgment.

Advisory Committee Comment—2012 Amendment

Rule 77.04 is amended to permit any notice required by the rule to be sent by electronic means in all cases. Although this will necessarily occur in cases using mandatory e-filing and e-service, the rule permits court administrators to use e-mail or electronic noticing in any other case where it is feasible.

Notice is required to be provided to the last known address of the party or attorney. The burden is squarely on the party or attorney to advise the court of any change in address. This rule should be read in conjunction with Rule 13.02 of the General Rules of Practice which permits the court administrator to discontinue providing postal notice where that last known address is known to be obsolete, typically by the return of prior mailings by the postal service.

RULES 78 AND 79. (RESERVED FOR FUTURE USE.)

RULE 80. STENOGRAPHIC REPORT OR TRANSCRIPT AS EVIDENCE

Whenever the testimony of a witness at a trial or hearing which was stenographically reported is admissible in evidence at a later trial, it may be proved by a reading of the transcript thereof duly certified by the person who reported the testimony. Such evidence is rebuttable and not conclusive.

RULE 81. APPLICABILITY; IN GENERAL

81.01. Statutory and Other Procedures

(a) **Procedures Preserved.** These rules do not govern pleadings, practice and procedure in the statutory and other proceedings listed in Appendix A insofar as they are inconsistent or in conflict with the rules.

(b) **Procedures Abolished.** [Abrogated].

(c) **Statutes Superseded.** Subject to provision (a) of this rule, the statutes listed in Appendix B and all other statutes inconsistent or in conflict with these rules are superseded insofar as they apply to pleading, practice, and procedure in the district court.

(Amended effective January 1, 1997.)

Advisory Committee Comments--1996 Amendments

Rule 81.01(b) should be abrogated to reflect the decision of the Minnesota Supreme Court in Rice v. Connolly, 488 N.W.2d 241, 244 (Minn. 1992), in which the court held: "We have determined that quo warranto jurisdiction as it once existed in the district court must be reinstated and that petitions for the writ of quo warranto and information in the nature of quo warranto shall be filed in the first instance in the district court." The court recognized its retention of original jurisdiction under Minnesota Statutes, section 480.04 (1990), and also indicated its "future intention to exercise that discretion in only the most exigent of circumstances. We comment further that the reinstatement of quo warranto jurisdiction in the district court is intended to exist side by side with the appropriate alternative forms of remedy heretofore available...." 488 N.W.2d at 244. The continued existence of a rule purporting to recognize a procedural remedy now expressly held to exist can only prove misleading or confusing in future litigation. Abrogation of the rule is appropriate to obviate any lack of clarity.

Although Rule 81.01(a) is not amended, the committee recommends that the list of special proceedings exempted from the rules by this rule be updated. An updated Appendix A is included in these proposed amendments.

81.02. Appeals to District Courts

These rules do not supersede the provisions of statutes relating to appeals to the district courts.

81.03. Rules Incorporated into Statutes

Where any statute heretofore or hereafter enacted, whether or not listed in Appendix A, provides that any act in a civil proceeding shall be done in the manner provided by law, such act shall be done in accordance with these rules.

RULE 82. JURISDICTION AND VENUE

These rules shall not be construed to extend or limit the jurisdiction of the district courts of Minnesota or the venue of actions therein.

RULE 83. RULES BY DISTRICT COURTS

Any court may recommend rules governing its practice not in conflict with these rules or with the General Rules of Practice for the District Courts, and those rules shall become effective as ordered by the Supreme Court.

(Amended effective January 1, 1992.)

Task Force Comment--1991 Adoption

This rule replaces existing Minn. R. Civ. P. 83. The purpose of this rule is to insure a mechanism to maintain uniformity in the local rules. The Task Force believes it is imperative that some method be enforced to provide for uniformity of rules that may be adopted in the future. This rule will allow either local rules, or statewide rules based on proposed local rules, and will permit the Supreme Court to review and coordinate the adoption of those rules. In the absence of this provision, uniformity would be achieved on the day these rules are adopted, but would disappear as soon as one court adopted a rule to supplement or vary the new Code of Rules.

The American Bar Association Standards Relating to Court Administration also favor the promulgation of uniform rules of practice issued by a central court. Standard 1.11(c) provides:

(c) Uniform standards of justice. The procedures by which the court system administers justice should be based on principles applicable throughout the system, and, so far as practicable, should be uniform in their particulars. The court system should have:

(i) Uniform rules of procedure, promulgated by a common authority;

(ii) Rules of court administration that are uniform so far as possible and have local variations only as approved by an appropriate central authority in the court system;

ABA Standards Relating to Court Administration, Standard 1.11(c)(i) & (ii) (1990).

RULE 84. APPENDIX OF FORMS

The forms contained in the Appendix of Forms sufficiently reflect the rules and are intended to indicate the simplicity and brevity of statement which the rules contemplate.

RULE 85. TITLE

These rules are known and cited as Rules of Civil Procedure.

RULE 86. EFFECTIVE DATE

86.01. Effective Date and Application to Pending Proceedings

(a) These rules as originally adopted took effect on January 1, 1952. They govern all proceedings and actions brought after that effective date, and also all further proceedings in actions then pending, except to the extent that in the opinion of the court their application in a particular action pending when the rules take effect would not be feasible, or would work injustice, in which event the procedure existing at the time the action was brought applies.

(b) Unless otherwise specified by the court, all amendments will take effect on either January 1 or July 1 in the year of or the year following their adoption. They govern all proceedings in actions brought after they take effect, and also all further proceedings in actions then pending, except as to the extent that in the opinion of the court their application in a particular action pending when the amendments take effect would not be feasible, or would work injustice, in which event the former procedure applies.

Made in the USA
Monee, IL
28 December 2021

87442738R00085